Assessing Vendors

Assessing Vendors

A Hands-On Guide to Assessing Infosec and IT Vendors

Josh More

ELSEVIER

AMSTERDAM • BOSTON • HEIDELBERG • LONDON
NEW YORK • OXFORD • PARIS • SAN DIEGO
SAN FRANCISCO • SINGAPORE • SYDNEY • TOKYO
Syngress is an imprint of Elsevier

SYNGRESS.

Acquiring Editor: Chris Katsaropoulos
Development Editor: Benjamin Rearick
Project Manager: Mohanambal Natarajan

Syngress is an imprint of Elsevier
225 Wyman Street, Waltham, MA 02451, USA

First published 2013

Notices
Knowledge and best practice in this field are constantly changing. As new research and experience broaden our understanding, changes in research methods, professional practices, or medical treatment may become necessary.

Practitioners and researchers must always rely on their own experience and knowledge in evaluating and using any information, methods, compounds, or experiments described herein. In using such information or methods they should be mindful of their own safety and the safety of others, including parties for whom they have a professional responsibility.

To the fullest extent of the law, neither the Publisher nor the authors, contributors, or editors, assume any liability for any injury and/or damage to persons or property as a matter of products liability, negligence or otherwise, or from any use or operation of any methods, products, instructions, or ideas contained in the material herein.

British Library Cataloguing-in-Publication Data
A catalogue record for this book is available from the British Library

Library of Congress Cataloging-in-Publication Data
A catalog record for this book is available from the Library of Congress

ISBN: 978-0-12-409607-3

For information on all Syngress publications
visit our website at www.syngress.com

This book has been manufactured using Print On Demand technology. Each copy is produced to order and is limited to black ink. The online version of this book will show color figures where appropriate.

CONTENTS

ACKNOWLEDGMENTS

This book evolved out of a presentation made at DerbyCon, so I would like to first thank the unnamed voting board of DerbyCon 2 for choosing a wacky joke talk about pens.

I would like to thank Kevin Riggins, my technical editor on this book. As this process applies very differently to small business and large enterprises, his input was extremely valuable.

I would also like to thank Anthony J. Stieber for contributing the page on assessing Cryptography. This topic alone could make its own book, so I greatly appreciate the work it took to condense it to a single page.

I would like to thank the SANS Community for being willing to review a beta version of this book, so I could address glaring holes and clarify areas of uncertainty. Specifically, I would like to thank Stephen Snyder, Wes Earnest, Fred Kerby, and Perry Straw. Though not (yet) a member of the community, I would also like to thank Mike Eck who provided similar insight.

Finally, all graphics in this book were made with the open source tools LibreOffice, Inkscape, and The Gimp. A big thank you goes out to the multitude of programmers who volunteered years of development to make these tools what they are and to release them for free for everyone.

INTRODUCTION

It always irritates me when a book starts with a justification of its own existence, so it somewhat surprises me to be starting this book in this manner. However, we face many issues today that must be addressed. Vendor selection processes fail when an organization keeps a wrong vendor too long and fails to adapt to changing circumstances. These processes fail when a needed vendor is not selected because the selection process becomes bogged down in trivialities. They fail when mature organizations select immature vendors who are simply unable to provide what they promise.

Vendor management is something of a black art in the IT industry. Those who are most successful either don't follow a process or keep their processes secret. Some people seem to intrinsically know which vendors are worth working with and which ones are not. They know how to choose technologies without getting bogged down in analysis and without escaping to a level of superficiality that would come back to bite them, two very common sources of vendor management failure.

As people observed how some organizations were highly successful in managing their vendors, bringing their projects to completion within their budget, and others were failing to implement technology profitably (or at all), vendor management requirements began to be included in various standards and regulations. The assumption seems to be that if regulations and standards such as HIPAA or PCI require that people pay attention to vendors, these failures will just work themselves out. Sadly, that does not seem to be the case.

That's why this book exists.

After first trying to find a workable vendor assessment process and then slowly building one of my own, it is time for me to let others in to the secret. I have, like many others in this industry, been forced to implement technologies based on other people's mid-guided decisions. I've made my own poor decisions and gotten myself and others stuck in the process. I've tried to make better decisions by putting increasing analytics around the process only to find the analysis process itself cause us to miss the project timeline. Finally, after over a decade, I've pieced together an approach that balances the need to find a good enough technology (product or service) without expending too many resources (time or money) getting there. I hope that my process will be of use to you.

All robust information assurance processes and regulations aside, successful vendor management involves a wide range of skills, from technical assessment to business communication to negotiation and covers many issues outside the scope of this book. Instead of trying to cover the world, this book focuses largely on the initial assessment process, with a goal to select a vendor to solve a specific problem that the organization is experiencing, improving an existing process or adding new capabilities. This book will touch on most of the skills needed to create a vendor management program, but will not delve very deeply into the continued operation aspects of such a program.

So why is vendor assessment needed?

Vendors engage in sales processes a whole lot more often than individuals do ... so they have a lot more practice at it. This results in a situation that is heavily tilted against buyers. Marketers are experts in manipulating how products are positioned and, because no product is perfect, there are many pressures against letting buyers run truly independent tests. Simultaneously, buyers must do more with less, so products positioned as time savers are more likely to be purchased.

Thus, we have developed a market in which both sides, the buyers and the vendors, are pressed for time and technology is increasingly positioned as "magical." Even though everyone involved knows how ridiculous it is, the trend continues, because to do otherwise would slow down the cycles and allow competition to get a leg up on us.

That's why I developed this vendor assessment process.

This book introduces a process by which you may rapidly find vendor candidates, filter out those that don't apply, and get to where you have a small number of choices to assess more deeply. The process involves determining assessment dimensions and then engaging in one or more cycles to manage the filtering process. It will touch on price negotiation and long-term operations, but fundamentally, it is about the assessment portion of your overall vendor management process.

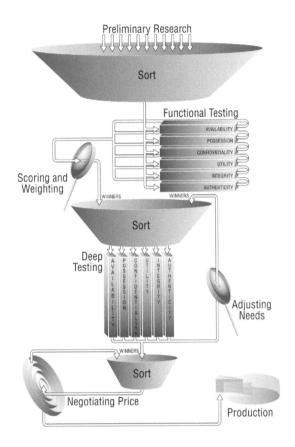

Here you can see that the process begins with a Preliminary Research phase, which gathers together various options and helps you to build selection criteria. These options are then filtered through a Sort process so obvious non-contenders can be removed from further consideration. Once a reasonable list of candidates is ready, the process moves along to Functional Testing.

Functional Testing involves running the same basic analysis against each candidate. The intent is to be fast, but fair. This phase of the process is very time-driven and, more than any other, aims for something approaching full coverage. Once this phase is completed, the candidates are Scored and Weighted and those that pass the tests, the "winners", move through the second Sort.

By this point, there will be only a small number of vendor candidates remaining, so they can reviewed in greater detail. This Deep Testing focuses on live verification of actual technical claims and, if any flaws are detected, ways to mitigate them. If clear winners are determined here, they get ranked in the final Sort process so you may begin Negotiating Price. If no clear winners are detected, the flaws in the analysis are identified and rectified and this phase of the process is re-run.

Once you finally have a preferred candidate and some backup options, it's time to Negotiate Price. For many vendors, price is extremely flexible, so it often doesn't take much in the way of negotiation to finish up the process and move along to Production. If, however, the primary candidate cannot meet your pricing needs, you can rerun this phase of the process again for the backup options. Then, in the end, you wind up with a vendor, product, and/or service that are good enough to meet your needs at a good enough price, so you can move on to Production.

In the end, you must choose a tool that works, but one that also feels right as you use it. You must choose a vendor that can technically support you, but also one that you trust both today and into the future. Attempts to standardize the process often fail due to choices that look correct in theory but feel wrong in practice. Thus, instead of choosing the *best* solution, this book is about choosing a *good* one. Choosing "good" is a much faster process than pursuing "best" (which often doesn't exist), and as technology and businesses change over time, the process results in a more flexible way in which vendors can be added and removed to your organization.

This book does not apply equally to all organizations. While the process itself will function in any size business, some businesses are structured such that any one person cannot be present for all phases of the process. As a rule of thumb, the larger your organization is, the fewer phases you may be involved in.

In large organizations, there are additional constraints beyond the relatively simple considerations of finding a vendor that provides "good enough" products or services. The cost structures of working at massive scale often force you into choosing a smaller set of vendors that are already approved by a vetting process. The political nature of working with multiple levels of people can force a predetermined vendor to win the selection process. You may also be given a set of criteria from a different team and won't be able to select your own criteria. In many cases, in fact, the process is not to choose the best vendor but to simply provide a "go/no go" decision for a particular vendor.

In extremely small organizations, you may well be bound more by time than any other factor. If this is the case, the entire process may be overly burdensome for decisions that must be made very quickly. Money will, of course, always be a factor, but if you don't have the time to make a well-researched decision, time concerns will override those of money.

Finally, in purpose-driven nonprofit organizations, financial concerns may not a factor at all. While there are far more nonprofit organizations running on shoe string budgets, there is a class of organization, often governmental, that has no budget concerns at all. In these organizations, the concern is solving the problem at hand and not negotiating over price.

Thus, if you do not have the ability to actually select vendors to feed into the assessment process, you should start reading at Functional Testing. If you are expected to provide a straightforward "go/no go" decision for a vendor, you should stop reading at the end of Deep Testing. If you are just expected to provide relative risk scores for vendors, start at Functional Testing and stop at Weighting and Scoring or Adjusting Needs, depending on how deep your company needs you to go.

If you are extremely bound by time, you may wish to skip Deep Testing and Adjusting Needs entirely and jump straight from Scoring and Weighting to Pricing and Negotiation. This will result in a less-well-tuned choice, but if you are blocked by time constraints by making the choice properly, you'll still be picking the best option available to you.

Finally, if you are not involved with pricing and are focused strictly on how well a solution will address a particular problem, you should stop reading at the end of Adjusting Needs. There is no need to get into the intricacies of pricing and negotiation if you won't be negotiating at all.

In all of these cases, of course, you risk making a decision on a vendor that won't address your issues very well. If you can't drive the process and alter the criteria based on what you find, you can't tune the vendor's offering to your precise needs. If you are stuck buying from a preapproved vendor with whom you have a site license, you are cutting off a wide range of options, often newer vendors who have a better value proposition. If you must decide simply whether or not to renew a product and there is great political pressure to renew, it could be career limiting to decide otherwise.

However, if this is the situation you are in, you are not actually being tasked with selecting a good vendor. You are being tasked with maintaining the status quo. While no one needs a book for that, it might help you to read the entire process so you can better understand your own organization's failings and prepare to do better at your next job.

Preliminary Research

1.1 PRELIMINARY RESEARCH

1.1.1 Identifying Vendorspaces

Vendors tend to create spaces for themselves in markets. This makes it easier for prospects to find them, but it also restricts the way in which you think about them. A vendor solidly branded in one "vendorspace" is less likely to be considered outside of it, regardless of how well they may fit other needs. This is made worse by analysis firms who like to say things such as "Vendor X should pick a market and dominate it instead of trying to be everything to everybody." So, while vendorspaces can be very useful in identifying candidates, keep in mind that the goal in selecting a vendor is to meet a business need, not to pick the "best" candidate on someone else's list.

In most cases, you will be searching within a well-known vendorspace, such as "disk encryption vendors" or "intrusion prevention vendors." However, vendorspaces have life spans. For example, text-based word processing tools were once incredibly popular, however, that vendorspace has contracted and the winners, Microsoft Word and WordPerfect, were migrated into graphical user interfaces. Along the way, tools like AppleWorks and WordStar died out. Thus, if you are exploring a vendorspace that is near the beginning or end of its life cycle, your choices within that space will be more limited and you may need to look further afield to solve your problem. Knowing this will help you identify when you have a reasonably complete list of candidates.

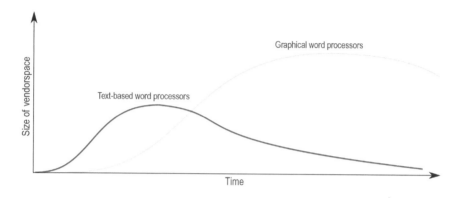

Vendorspace lifetimes vary with the type of solution and in relation to other competing vendorspaces.

Vendorspaces near their end are fairly easy to identify. Any technology that is referred to as "old school," "legacy," or "dead" likely reflects a contracting vendorspace. This isn't necessarily bad; after all, there are still a lot of people using legacy mainframe technology. However, there will likely be few newcomers in those spaces, so you can shortcut this phase of the process as there will be less discovery involved.

Vendorspaces near the beginning of their rise are harder to work with. Not only are there not many vendors in them, but there will be significant disagreement between vendors as to whether or not they are in the space and whether that space even exists. At the time of this writing, the Unified Threat Management (UTM) and Next Generation FireWall (NGFW) vendorspaces have effectively merged and a new "Intelligent Threat Management" (ITM) vendorspace may be beginning to emerge. This means that while vendors such as Fortinet, Sophos, Watchguard, and PaloAlto fight with one another for dominance over the merged UTM/NGFW vendorspace, other vendors such as Barrier1 and MetaFlows choose not to compete there and instead are creating the new ITM vendorspace. This happens because, as these firms provide innovative approaches to problems, they are not exactly NGFWs or UTMs and may look fairly rough when compared to polished examples from those vendorspaces. However, because their own vendorspace hasn't fully materialized yet, their new capabilities aren't truly understood by prospective customers.

The primary rule in vendor assessment and selection is to always keep your needs first in mind. Then, if one vendorspace doesn't clearly solve your problems, you will have to consider several and look to the overlap. Before you can start exploring, you'll need a map. To make this map, consider all ways that your problem can be solved and build a list of possible solution types. This will help guide you to specific vendorspaces, so you can decide which ones you will be focusing upon.

1.1.2 Identifying Candidates

The first step in any assessment process is to try to gather as many candidates as possible. Looking at vendorspaces can be a good guide for candidates, but it should not be the only one. Because the assessment process operates as a funnel, continuously filtering out unacceptable options, the more options you put in the top, the more certain you will be of the final result. It is important, in doing this, to not limit yourself to only a single solution class. If your business is hostile to open source, those solutions may not be ideal. However, if they work for your purposes and none of the proprietary options do, they might wind up being the best choice from a set of imperfect solutions. You should also consider options that are either partial or overly-complete. Many "suite" solutions do far more than you might need to solve your problem, but this isn't a reason to exclude them. This is a point of price negotiation later in the process.

To develop the full list, you must pull from many sources. The so-called "independent" analysis firms tend to use vendorspaces to compare technologies. Thus, once we've identified the name the market assigns to the type of solution we need, we can search for lists of options in that space. For example, suppose you were looking to compare Intrusion Prevention Systems, your first place to check may be Wikipedia. Then you can check for lists from Gartner, Forrester, and IDC. Most of these lists are pay-only, but the firms that score well tend to promote the fact in their press releases, so even if you can't get the report itself, you can often get the list of the firms on the report. Press releases can be searched at http://www.pressreleasespider.com/.

Give yourself 5 minutes to build a list from Wikipedia, then 10 minutes each to search out vendors in the space from each of the top three analysis firms.

A Note on "Independent" Analysis Firms

As you do this step of the analysis, do not fall into the trap of thinking that these big-name research firms are the final word in the space. Remember, all you are doing is identifying candidates.

These firms require a lot of money to operate and, because of this, they charge vendors to participate in their studies. Some of them even have a "preassessment" service that lets the vendors pay even more money to help the analysis firms set up the technology to maximize their score in the tests. Because of this, you cannot trust that the list is complete (some vendors choose to not participate) and you cannot trust that the scores are fair (as some vendors do not pay for preassessment help).

Additionally, as the assessment firms are focusing on a general case, there is no way that they can know your particular needs, so even if the list were complete and the score were accurate, there is no way to tell how well it would apply to what you need. Thus, these reports are good sources from which to build lists as well as being good sources of concerns about a technology or business. They are not necessarily good places from which to pull your final choice.

Once you have your initial list of names, it's time to fill in further. This is where search engines come in. A good way to do this is to actually look at the ads. Vendors who want to enter a market will pay for online advertising, so if you just search on a topic and turn off your ad-blocker, you can fill in your list.

As an example, suppose you are searching for an Intrusion Prevention System, you need to build a list of keywords. Luckily, Google makes this easy for you. Go to their keyword tool (https://adwords.google.com/o/KeywordTool) and search on "IPS," "Intrusion Prevention Systems." This feeds back 100 keyword terms, including "intrusion prevention software," "ips monitor," and "network intrusion detection." Go through the list and pull out all the ones that seem to work well. Keep the list manageable. At this stage, I don't like to go over 20 terms, but your numerical limit may be different. Selecting too few terms results in not feeding enough candidates into the process. Selecting too many means that you spend more time than is necessary doing searches. If you don't have your own rough limit yet, a good rule of thumb is to start at one term and keep doing searches until you do several searches in a row that don't identify new candidates. Your numerical limit will be lower than that.

For example, at the time of writing this, the tool suggested the following:

Google Keyword Search: "Intrusion Prevention System"		
wireless intrusion prevention	intrusion detection systems	host intrusion prevention
intrusion protection system	network intrusion detection	firewall
cisco intrusion detection systems	Nids	host intrusion detection system
computer security	network security	intrusion prevention solution
intrusion prevention systems ips	wireless intrusion prevention	ips intrusion prevention system
intrusion detection	intrusion detection software	symantec intrusion prevention
sourcefire ips	free intrusion prevention system	linux intrusion prevention
host based intrusion detection	intrusion detection tools	best intrusion prevention system
network based intrusion	cisco intrusion prevention	intrusion prevention software

Clearly, some of these, such as "firewall" and "network security" are too general to be useful. However, this search alone points out that these devices tend to come in three flavors: Network, Wireless, and Host-based, that there are free options that could be considered, and that Cisco, Sourcefire, and Symantec are likely established and well-known vendors in this vendorspace.

Once you have the list, do a search on each term on an ad-supported search engine such as Google and Bing. Glance through the first few pages looking at both the results and the ads and fill in your list of potential vendors. This step in the process should take no more than an hour.

Extending this search on Google and Bing for the terms "Intrusion Detection System," "Intrusion Prevention System," and "NIDS" returns the following list of advertising vendors to consider:

Search Engine-Provided List of Vendors			
Arbor Networks	IBM	Real Time	Symantec
Check Point	ISS	SecureWorks	Trustwave
Cisco	Juniper	Smoothwall	TycoIS
Cyberoam	Manage Engine	Snort	Watchguard
GFI	Net Gladiator	Sophos	Zentyal
Gladiator	Nokia	Sourcefire	
HP	Radware	Spector360	

Some of these, of course, are likely false positives and reflect resellers of solutions and not the solutions themselves. However, those will be rapidly filtered out in the following steps. Like a brainstorming exercise, the goal here is to gather as many potentially useful names as possible.

Now, you've spent less than two hours and should have a reasonably complete set of names for future analysis. If you wish to go further, there are three optional methods that you can use to fill in the list further. As they involve one-on-one communication, these take additional time, but can do wonders if your list feels somewhat thin.

The first method is to pick a company you recognize and contact a sales person there. When they answer, tell them that you are considering their solution, but you have to look at two competing offerings. Ask what else you should consider. In this instance, the sales person will want to drive you toward solutions that they consider less good than theirs—after all, they want the sale. What's nice about this approach is that you are likely to get names that won't be on the analysis reports, as products that fail the "independent" tests don't tend to trumpet that fact on the Internet. If the reason for failure doesn't apply to your use case, it doesn't matter to you. The downside of this approach, of course, is that it gets you on the sales person's call list. While some will just contact you a couple of times and give up, others will hound you forever. It may be wise to use throw-away e-mail addresses if you take this approach.

The second method is to go to a user group or association, call a friendly competitor, or talk to other people in your area and just ask what you should consider. Most technical people have a mental list of cool tools they always wanted to play with but couldn't. These may not be suitable to your needs (or theirs), but as the goal is to fill in your list, this is a valid approach. You can often get more cutting/bleeding edge tools on your list this way.

The third method is something of a hybrid. Odds are that there are some Value-Added Resellers (VARs) in your area. Often, the technology that you are considering is resold by a VAR. Call each one of them, explain what you're doing, and ask if they have any vendors that should be on your list. Most VARs are friendly and will give you a list of technologies that they like. Sure, in the long run, they're going to want to make a sale, but because few VARs are limited to only a single vendor in each vendorspace, they're often willing and able to give you a bit of free guidance.

Once you are reasonably happy with your list, it's time to start analyzing and filtering.

1.1.3 Building Criteria

Now you have a list so it's tempting to run through it and start kicking off the vendors you know will fail, but that's premature. The problem is you don't yet know much about the options. The famous saying is that "no one ever got fired for buying IBM" (or whoever is the current winner in the space). However, no one ever got promoted doing that either. The goal is not find the least objectionable option. If it were, you wouldn't have bought this book; you'd have just let your sales person take you out to a nice dinner and then bought whatever they suggested. As noted earlier, the goal is to find technology or services that will help you either do something entirely new or improve an existing process.

To meet this goal, you have to stop guessing. You need solid data. However, solid data is hard to come by without doing full implementations of every technology. By this point, your list is likely between 20 and 50 items long and no one has time to do that many proof-of-concept implementations. You must weed the list down to size, but you can't run the risk of possibly cutting out an ideal choice. You need metrics and a data-driven approach for making your decision. Luckily, data has different thresholds.

At the most surface-level, all you know is that other people are using the technology to solve a problem similar to what you are facing. That's enough to get them on the list. Now, you need to identify at a deeper level, what exactly the vendors do. You do not, at this point, need to know how they do it or how well they do it. All you're doing is building another list—this one of features. If you are starting from scratch, this list will drive the assessment directly. If, however, you are in a larger organization and have been provided with a list of features and told to find a tool, this process will serve as a check against your list, so you can revise your comparison list before you go too far down this road.

Now, it's seldom wise to buy something based on untested features but knowing what a tool does is useful. The average person doesn't need to know the difference between a claw hammer, a ball pein hammer, and a cross pein pin hammer. After all, each of them pounds nails just fine. However, if you dig into the features, you learn that one of them is good for cabinets, another is good for metal work, and another for building decks. The ideal tool will depend on your specific use case but listing the features of each tool will help you tune your case to better fit what you need to do.

Claw hammer   Ball pein hammer   Cross pein pin hammer

Stop! Hammer time!: Illustration of different types of tools.

For this, simply go to the home page of each option on your list and begin building a list of interesting features. You're not ranking vendors or features at this point; you just want the basic list. Odds are, at the end of the process, it will be about twice as long as your original list of candidates. Spend about 5 minutes on each candidate, otherwise your research process will likely run away from you and you'll have a greater chance of falling for the marketing hype on the Web sites. Maintain individual lists of features for each option and then combine them later. This makes it very easy to quickly identify a candidate's capabilities if you need to later in the process.

As you go through this process, you may find that specific vendors aren't what you thought they were and have no chance whatsoever of helping you solve your problem. Feel free to exclude those vendors at this point but do not exclude any others.

Once you have the basic list, if you need additional features, you can take advantage of the fact that many vendorspaces are structured to work within the VAR environment. In this environment, the vendors have to arm the resellers to sell their wares. This is typically done through the use of "battlecards" that directly compare the vendor to their competition. Unfortunately, these battlecards are usually licensed for internal use only and are not made available to customers and prospects. Fortunately, many VARs ignore the licensing issue and make them available on the Web. A simple Google search on "<VendorName> battlecard filetype:pdf" will often turn up a pile of references for <VendorName> that detail frank information about that vendor's strengths and weaknesses as compared to their competitors. Simply repeat this search for each vendor on your candidate list and expand your feature list.

A word of warning—this search approach may be considered unethical or illegal in certain contexts. If you work within an environment that has strict restrictions on where you can get your information (somewhat common in "open bid" government situations), you may wish to avoid this method and instead fill in the feature list by reading articles to glean what you can. This will be slower but ethically cleaner than the other search process.

Once you have your feature list, you need to go through it and score each feature according to "Required," "Would Be Nice," "Doesn't Matter," and "Do Not Want." Be careful not to put too many into the "Doesn't Matter" category. People have a tendency to lump things into a general category if they don't want to think about it. As a rule of thumb, if more than 25% of your feature list winds up in "Doesn't Matter," you haven't thought about it enough.

This is how you can begin building a table of anticipatory metrics, or if a list has already been provided to you, revising your existing table. Simply list all of your "Required" items in a table, all of your "Would Be Nice" in another table, and your "Do Not Want"s in yet another. Then, as you go through research or functional testing steps, you can fill in these tables.

PHASE 2

Sort

2.1 SORT

2.1.1 Quick Sort—Filter Out

The quick sort phase focuses on eliminating candidates from consideration. For some projects, this may be combined with the next phase, but for the sake of simplicity, they are separate in this book. As you know what features are required, you can do a very quick, rough sort by throwing out all candidates that do not include all of your required features. Because you've kept the feature lists of each option, this should be extremely fast. You should be able to complete the quick sort in less than an hour.

It is also common to wind up with no vendors or a very small set of vendors that meet your requirements. If this occurs, it is likely that your "Required" features are unrealistic. You need to decide if you will adjust your requirements and live with less than you thought you needed, or if you want to explore ways in which products could be combined to meet your needs. If you choose the latter, you need to reconsider the vendorspace(s) in which you are looking. If you are combining two products to meet a need, you must run through this process twice. A common example is that of disk encryption. It would be nice if disk encryption technologies had a two-factor authentication feature, but that's still very rare in that particular vendorspace. So, if you need encrypted laptops that require people to log in with a password and a keyfob, you would have to run one vendor assessment project on disk encryption and one vendor assessment project on two-factor OS authentication.

A good rule of thumb is to have your Required feature list loose enough that the quick sort only knocks out up to 20% of your candidates. That way you can determine actual fits from functional testing and will not be fully reliant on what vendors say on their web sites.

2.1.2 Quick Sort—Filter In

Of those vendors remaining on your list, you should now go through your feature requirements again and mark them according to each feature category. This is easily done in a spreadsheet. Just run all vendor features on your list along the left-hand column, prefaced with "R-" for "Required," "WBN-" for "Would Be Nice," "DM-" for "Doesn't Matter," and "DNW-" for "Do Not Want." Then run all vendors across the first row and start noting which vendors have which features.

It is tempting to skip this step, but keep in mind that desires shift during the assessment process. Just as some Required features may turn out not be required, features that might be nice can become Required and those that do not matter can start mattering. By having a standard table to which you can refer, you can quickly identify the ramifications of making a change. By using the Data→Sort capabilities in most spreadsheet programs, you can easily identify if the change in a feature requirement would drastically reduce or expand your space.

As actual vendor feature support can change rapidly, this example and those similar to this elsewhere in the book will use fake vendor names. It is even possible that vendor features will change during the course of your assessment. By maintaining these analysis spreadsheets, you can quickly pivot your assessment and include or exclude vendors as new information becomes available.

	Ausonius	Choliamb	Ennius	Epyllion	Lekythion	Martial	Neoteric	Status	Tibullus
R—Over 80% zero day protection	✓	✓	✓	✓	✓	✓	✓	✓	✓
R—Automatic malware removal	✓	✓	✓	✓	✓	✓	✓	✓	✓
R—Detects FakeAV	✓	✓	✓	✓	✓	✓	✓	✓	✓
R—Blocks malicious web sites	✓	✓	✓	✓	✓	✓	✓	✓	✓
R—Provides memory scanning	✓	✓	✓	✓	✓	✓	✓	✓	✓
R—Supports Windows XP	✓	✓	✓	✓	✓	✓	✓	✓	✓
R—Supports Windows 7	✓	✓	✓	✓	✓	✓	✓	✓	✓
R—Runs on 64 bit hardware	✓	✓	✓	✓	✓	✓	✓	✓	✓
R—Requires less than 1 Gb RAM	✓	✓	✓	✓	✓	✓	✓	✓	✓
R—Includes inbound firewall	✓	✓	✓	✓	✓	✓	✓	✓	✓
R—Integrates with Active Directory	✓	✓	✓	✓	✓	✓	✓	✓	✓
R—Integration with Syslog	✓	✓	✓	✓	✓	✓	✓	✓	✓
R—Provides DLP—Financial	✓	✓	✓	✓	✓	✓	✓	✓	✓
R—Centralized endpoint management	✓	✓	✓	✓	✓	✓	✓	✓	✓
R—Requires SQL Server 2005 +	✓	✓	✓	✓	✓	✓	✓	✓	✓
R—Uses internal list to control apps	✓	✓	✓	✓	✓	✓	✓	✓	✓
R—24/7 support available	✓	✓	✓	✓	✓	✓	✓	✓	✓
WBN—Supports AD user groups	✓	✓			✓	✓		✓	
WBN—Supports Windows 8				✓	✓				
WBN—Over 90% zero day protection	✓	✓	✓		✓	✓	✓	✓	
WBN—Over 95% zero day protection	✓	✓			✓	✓			
WBN—Approved by AV-Test.org	✓	✓	✓	✓	✓		✓	✓	✓
WBN—VB100 approved for Windows XP	✓	✓	✓	✓	✓	✓	✓	✓	✓

	Ausonius	Choliamb	Ennius	Epyllion	Lekython	Martial	Neoteric	Statius	Tibullus
WBN—VB100 approved for Windows 7	✓	✓		✓	✓	✓		✓	✓
WBN—Provides Patch Management	✓		✓	✓	✓			✓	
WBN—Requires one central console	✓	✓		✓	✓	✓			
WBN—Centralized management via web	✓				✓	✓			
WBN—Includes outbound firewall	✓				✓			✓	
WBN—Provides tamper protection	✓	✓		✓	✓	✓		✓	✓
WBN—Provides DLP—ID Numbers	✓		✓	✓	✓	✓	✓		
WBN—Provides DLP—Health	✓		✓	✓	✓	✓	✓		
WBN—Provides DLP—Custom	✓		✓				✓		
WBN—Integration with VMware vShield	✓				✓		✓	✓	
WBN—Requires SQL Server 2008 +	✓				✓	✓			
WBN—Supports OSX	✓	✓	✓		✓	✓		✓	
WBN—Requires less than 512 Mb RAM		✓	✓		✓	✓			
WBN—24/7 support standard		✓					✓		✓
DM—VB100 approved for Windows 8		✓			✓				
DM—Supports Linux	✓				✓				
DM—Integration with SNMP		✓		✓			✓	✓	
DM—Global presence evenly distributed		✓		✓			✓		
DM—Provides NAC	✓					✓			
DM—Centralized management via app						✓		✓	✓
DNW—Requires SQL Server 2012					✓				
DNW—Requires two + central consoles			✓				✓	✓	✓

Functional Testing

3.1 FUNCTIONAL TESTING

Once you've got the list slightly whittled, it's time to begin functional testing. The goal here is to check each technology or vendor against a common set of questions. These questions are best determined before every engagement, as attempts to predefine a general set of questions results in a general solution being chosen. Some questions, though, you already have. You know what features you need and which ones are nice. You know which features you do not want, so you can easily determine how easy the features you want are to use and how difficult the ones you do not want are to disable. The rest, though, is more of an art than a science. Like all arts, however, your skill will improve with practice.

Fundamentally, you are pursuing a solution to a problem, so whatever solution you choose must actually solve that problem. However, the reasons for failure go far beyond mere technical issues. In many cases, a technology can fail because it is rejected by the team using it, flaws in how it is implemented, and native problems with how the technology is designed. The user experience is often the most critical component of a successful deployment. As you begin to delve into the inner workings of a technology, you should consider these issues.

3.1.1 Choosing a System

At this point, it is best to select a set of guiding criteria to help you fairly assess each candidate. In general, what works best is to choose a small set of variables and ask "how does this technology compare to the other technologies according to variable 1?," then do the same for variable 2, variable 3, etc. There are as many ways to do this as there are people doing it. However, there are some common variable sets that work well. How well these variable sets work depend largely on the number of variables. Fewer variables cause you to risk insufficient coverage to make a good decision and too many can cause distraction, so you spent more time in the process than is necessary.

In the Security world, it is common to use either the C.I.A. triad or the CISSP domains.

The C.I.A. triad consists of Confidentiality, Integrity, and Availability. If you were using this system, you would run down each candidate and look at each variable, so you'd ask yourself questions like:

- Confidentiality
  - How does this system protect the stored data from being accessed by the wrong people?
  - How does the vendor operationally respond to events like other customers accessing our data?
- Integrity
  - How well can I rely on the data or functionality of the technology to be what I expect?
  - How reliable are the people who run the company? Can I trust them if things break?
- Availability
  - How reliable is the technology itself? What are the average uptime metrics?
  - If I have a problem, how quickly can I get support to help me with it?

These questions alternate focus between the technical and business issues, so you get a good overview of your vendors.

If you were taking the CISSP domain approach, you would be dealing with 10 different variables:

1. Access Control
2. Telecommunications and Network Security
3. Information Security Governance and Risk Management
4. Software Development Security
5. Cryptography
6. Security Architecture and Design
7. Security Operations
8. Business Continuity and Disaster Recovery Planning
9. Legal, Regulations, Investigations, and Compliance
10. Physical (Environmental) Security.

As you can see, you'll often get a lot more questions using this system; however, they wouldn't all necessarily apply for all vendorspaces. If, for example, you were buying software, you'd care about things like Access Control, Cryptography, and Software Development Security. However, Telecommunications and Physical Security might not matter enough to explore.

No matter how hard you try, you're never going to get 100% coverage on your analysis, so the important thing is to pick a variable system that gives you reasonable coverage without wasting too much of your time. In general, I find the C.I.A. system does not provide enough coverage and the CISSP system provides too much. When using the former, you can be led to select a poor vendor because you simply don't dig deep enough. When using the latter, a significant amount of time is wasted on paperwork and does not provide value to the process.

The limit is going to be the number of dimensions that you can hold in your head at any given time. This way, as you assess systems, you don't have to bounce between modes of thinking too much. This process, called "context shift," is a very common source of time loss when doing analyses. If you are running down a large list for each candidate, you have to constantly change your mode of thinking and every time you do, it will cost you a little bit of time. If your list is too short, you will be losing time thinking of real-world scenarios that could be concerning but cannot be captured in your limited system.

For me, the magic number is six. I've done reviews of technologies from a threat vector perspective and used the following categories:

1. Network Threats
2. Web Threats
3. Malware Threats
4. Application Control Issues
5. Data Loss Events
6. Trust.

This tends to work well if you are looking at data concerns as it flows into an environment, gets processed or modified, and potentially flows out. The "Trust" category covers the human interactions with the data, by customers, internal employees, or by outside vendors. The other variables cover the common types of attack against a data flow.

More generally and outside the security space, though, what I find works well is the Parkerian Hexad. In 2002, Donn B. Parker proposed the following as an update to the traditional C.I.A. model:

- Availability
- Possession/Control
- Confidentiality
- Utility
- Integrity
- Authenticity.

This expands the assessment space in a very useful way. Possession/Control focuses on issues that could result in exploitation of Confidence, Integrity, or Availability, so precursor issues don't have to be shoehorned into a poorly fitting category. Authenticity focuses on verification of Integrity, so you don't have to combine definitive breaches with potential breaches as they are handled very differently. Finally, Utility covers situations in which systems can be otherwise secure but are not useful. This is one of the most important assessment variables when looking at vendors, as it also covers situations in which the technology does everything it is supposed to do, but for political or technical reasons, it is not a good fit for your organization.

While any variable set will work this assessment process, the rest of this book will focus on the Parkerian Hexad as it is frequently a useful set of guiding variables.

3.1.2 Using Scales

Once you've chosen a system, you need to choose your scoring metrics. For each variable, you will assign each candidate a numerical score. These will be used to filter out "losers" and, possibly, to select winners. This will be done with Likert items. We're not actually practicing psychometrics here, so we don't need a full scale or to explore the details of the theories being used. If this interests you, just search on "Likert Scale" and spend about four hours following links and reading articles.

For our purposes, a Likert item is the sort of question you often see on surveys. Something like:

- How useful is this book?

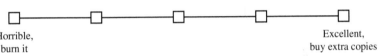

Horrible,
burn it Excellent,
buy extra copies

If you marked the rightmost box, you would score it as a five. The leftmost box would get scored as a one. Scoring in the middle, of course, would be a three. Typically, this would be combined with other questions which, at the end, would be averaged to get the answer you care about.

For our purposes, we just care about how well each option meets each of our six variables. This means that we would create questions for each variable that also cover all the features that matter to us. Then, we build our averages for each variable to get to the point in the analysis where we filter out more options.

As with choosing a variable system, there are many ways to build Likert items and Likert Scales. Many people like to use 10 choices for each item. This is the typical Internet survey you see questions such as "With 1 being awful and 10 being awesome, how much do you like cats?". However, resolution is a vitally important consideration. If you were asking a bunch of your friends how much they liked cats because you were curious, does the difference between an average score of 7 and an average score of 8 really matter? If you were asking a single person, perhaps your significant other, how much they liked cats because you were going to ask them to move in with you and Mister Fuzzy Flufflepants III, the subtle difference between a 4 and a 5 might be very important.

In general, you should pick as low a resolution as is useful to you. The smallest resolution is "2." This would be your typical questions that are answered either "yes" or "no." However, you've already used this in the first round asking the basic question "Does this vendor stand a chance of winning at all?" If not, they were excluded so you got to a smaller list of acceptable candidates. Thus, we need a great resolution for the rest of the assessment.

In most cases, 10 choices will be far too many as you would spend your time thinking things like: "Is it an 8 or 9?," "Maybe it's a 7?," "Maybe I should watch videos on YouTube while I think about this?".

This costs you a lot more time than the actual analysis.

Generally, four- or six-choice Likert items tend to be the most useful. By avoiding odd numbers, you also avoid the tendency for people to just check the middle option when a difficult decision must be made. Using an even set of options is called a "forced choice" and can be problematic in certain fields. However, for vendor assessment, reducing choice speeds up the process and seldom has a significant impact on the final result.

To keep things simple, the rest of this book will assume that you're using a six-choice model, as we want to force a choice, and the difference between "sorta liking, really liking, and loving," a feature matters within many corporate cultures.

Finally, for each question, assign a time value to reflect how much you care about the answer. This is not how much time you expect it will take to answer the question. This is the maximal amount of time that, if elapsed without an answer, means that you will assign the lowest value possible to the Likert item. This is a check to prevent you from wasting too much time on data gathering. Try to be fair in assigning these, as you are not trying to penalize vendors with which you have less familiarity, you are just trying to keep your time from slipping away from you.

3.1.3 Testing Availability

Aspects of vendor availability cover both that of the technology itself and of the vendor. Technological considerations should include the reliability of network connections, redundancy of the hardware to protect against component failure, and, if the solution is hosted, those locations for geographic redundancy. For most IT projects, the availability of the data should also be a concern. When comparing two products, of which only one has a data export feature, the presence of that feature should result in a higher data availability score as that will prevent future vendor lock-in. You should also review the availability of any portions of the environment on which the product would depend.

It is common for organizations to invest in a single appliance. If successful, that technology often gets deployed to production without further investment, so that vendor becomes a single point of failure. Thus, to protect against an availability failure, the final analysis should include redundancy for all vendors or for none. This keeps the analysis fair and keeps cost estimation in future phases fairly accurate.

In some cases, the availability of the source code should be considered as well. This may not be an important factor in all situations, but if you are counting the availability of support resources, the presence of the source code can go a long way toward mitigating concerns over lack of official support in open source technology or for proprietary systems that offer code escrow services.

Support is, of course, a critical factor. On the nontechnological side of the analysis, you should call support and see how long it takes to get a response. Contact other customers of the vendor and see what they think of speed (Availability) and accuracy (Utility) of the support system. Don't place trust in legacy metrics around support availability. While most vendors are fairly stable metric-wise, support levels shift quickly and seldom in positive directions. If a vendor starts to experience great success in the market, support often weakens as it takes time to rebuild to an acceptable level. Similarly, if a vendor starts to lose business, support is often cut so they can focus in other areas. It is important to periodically test this.

You should also test the support bypass system. Few vendors admit that these exist, but almost all vendors allow you to jump straight to an engineer by complaining to your salesperson. Check this by calling your salesperson and asking to schedule a ten-minute call with one of their sales engineers. Good vendors will get you something in a day or two. Excellent vendors will get you something that day. Vendors that take longer or force you to work within the system are likely insufficiently nimble. This reflects poorly on their ability to service you, but also on their ability to react to changes in the market. As you shift into a full vendor management system, this is another area where you may wish to conduct periodic testing.

To start down this path, create a testing table for this variable of analysis and segment the questions to identify questions about the technology and about the vendor's business model (nontechnical) and further break those apart into those questions that you can answer with research and those that require some level of direct contact with the system (demo system or proof of concept). Finally, figure out how much the answer to that question is worth to you in terms of time, so if the time elapses without you learning the answer, you can give that question a failing score and move on.

Testing Table—Availability

Technology—Research
  • How available is the source code? (5 min)
  • How much throughput does the solution handle? (5 min)

Technology—Hands On
  • How does the system support multiple simultaneous users? (5 min)
  • How does the system respond to crafted loops in the process flow? (15 min)

Nontechnical—Research
  • How responsive do existing customers say the vendor is during emergencies? (30 min)
  • How many alternate support paths exist in the event that standard support is overwhelmed? (5 min)

Nontechnical—Hands On
  • How long does it take for support to answer the phone? (5 min)
  • How long does it take until support returns a message/e-mail? (5 min/24 h)

3.1.4 Testing Possession/Control

For some vendors, this variable may not apply well. If you are considering a solution that is 100% cloud across the entire vendorspace, then everyone will likely score similarly. If, however, you have a fundamental choice between cloud and locally-hosted options or between public and private cloud options, physical control over the system will be a factor. How important a factor this is will be determined later. Right now, you are focusing on gathering data, not making decisions.

At a logical control level, you should be concerned about who has control over your system. In the case of an appliance, this would likely be your own people and anyone on the vendor's side that might have support access, so that should be verified. There have been instances where vendors release products with backdoors in them that allow outsiders to take control via a support account. Thus, it's important to understand how the vendor may have access to your systems, so you can take it away if you so choose.

If you are looking at software, you should find out how the update approval process works. In most cases, getting updates from the vendors is great, and you should trust their ability to maintain their systems. However, in high-risk environments, such updates may need to be tested first, so you may wish to score the vendor along those lines. For instance, if the reception of an unplanned update could cause a critical failure, that event should be thought of as a high concern.

Finally, if you are looking at cloud solutions, consider whether the lack of control is an issue. For some things, such as spam filtering, it may not matter. After all, e-mail from the Internet is effectively public and it makes little difference whose servers the mail flows through. Having one more hop in the mail path isn't going to harm you much and having experts able to filter it for you is a strong benefit. However, hosting all of your e-mail on a cloud solution may involve more risk than you can accept.

On the nontechnical side, this is where you dig into vendor partnership arrangements. Few vendor technologies are 100% comprised of their own technologies. Web and e-mail filters are often outsourced. Processing engines are licensed from other firms and there is always the risk that a critical component may be outside the control of either you or your vendor. There may be little that you can practically do about this if all vendors in the space work that way. However, if some vendors do everything themselves and others do not, it can be a critical factor. It can also point to areas in which the do-it-all vendors may fail in other variables, as it is rare for any vendor to do everything themselves and do it well.

An example of this is that of patch management. At the time of this writing, there are numerous patch management solutions in the market. However, many of them license technology from a company called Lumension. This means that if you purchase Dell Kace, Forescout, Novell Zenworks, or Sophos (among others), you are getting Lumension technology to manage patches. If Lumension were to experience a problem, it is possible that it would affect all of the vendors that use them. So, you should check what controls the vendor has over bad data or bad actions on the part of their partners.

Testing Table—Possession/Control
Technology—Research 　• How much third-party technology does the solution encompass? (15 min) 　• How does the vendor's backdoor support access system function? (15 min)
Technology—Hands On 　• How easily can an admin-level user take over another admin user's account? (30 min) 　• How easily can you, as an owner, block the vendor from accessing the system? (30 min)
Nontechnical—Research 　• How robust is the vendor's plan for situations in which their technology partners suffer a failure? (30 min) 　• How many historical events have occurred in which an outsider has taken over the vendor's system? (15 min)
Nontechnical—Hands On 　• How easily can you get the support personnel to reset your password on the demo account? (15 min) 　• How easily can you impersonate a technology partner to affect a system update? (1 h)

3.1.5 Testing Confidentiality

Confidentiality is the measurement of how likely something is to stay safe from the prying eyes of others. When comparing vendors, it is common to hear "our stuff is secure" with almost no details. As you test confidentiality, keep in mind that more than any other variable here, you will be misled by vendors. This is not always intentional. A common example is encryption.[1] If a product uses encryption, most sales people promote it as completely secure. However, a true measure of confidentiality in this case would involve user access and key management. There have also been cases where encryption is technically in use, but is using null or weak keys, so little actual protection is provided. If the sales people don't understand the product well enough to explain how it works, you must either talk to someone who does or figure it out yourself. Hands-on testing is often essential for verifying confidentiality. In this phase, you can best do this with a demo or test VM. In a later phase, you'll have the chance to dig more deeply.

If you are assessing an open source technology, you can verify confidentiality by reviewing the code. For all systems, see if you can browse to data on the file system, bypassing the application entirely.

---

[1]More on testing for cryptography can be found at the end of Phase 5.

Try to bypass authentication or read data before it is encrypted. Many encryption-based confidentiality failures occur when a user's account and password are guessed and the data is accessed legitimately. Others happen when the data is copied into RAM. Still others happen when the encryption system fails and the data is written into a temporary file. If, at any point, you can access data as a user that should not have access, the confidentiality score should be reduced.

At a nontechnical level, it's harder. You can try to socially engineer the vendor's support team to reset a password for you or just ask them what their process is. You can ask them to tell you how their audit logs function so you can detect if someone's password is reset or their account is accessed in a nontraditional way. However, fully and formally analyzing the confidentiality of a system takes a lot more time than it's worth at this stage of the game. After all, if you can exclude others and wind up with a short list of three or four options that win with different variables, you may not need to get into this at all.

Testing Table—Confidentiality
Technology—Research • What level of encryption is in use to protect the data? (5 min) • What model does the system use for password resets? (5 min)
Technology—Hands On • How easily can you, with one user's account, read the data in another user's account? (15 min) • How easy is it to manipulate session data to take over another user's account? (30 min)
Nontechnical—Research • How many vulnerabilities have there been in the last 5 years that, if exploited, exposed user data? (15 min) • How much internal vendor data can you collect with targeted search engine queries? (15 min)
Nontechnical—Hands On • How much information does the vendor provide about "reference" clients? (5 min) • How much information about your organization do vendor employees not directly connected to this project know? (10 min)

3.1.6 Testing Utility

This is often the most critical variable for a vendor assessment. Simply put, you are measuring whether the technology works as you expect and whether your organization can actually use it. If the technology doesn't seem to work and the vendor isn't helping you with issues, stop the analysis for that vendor and move on. If the people don't like the technology and they like another one that is comparable, you don't need to go any further. If the vendor is difficult to work with (slow to answer questions, hard to find the right person) and there is a viable alternative, you can pursue that. A low score in Utility is more likely to exclude an option than one in any other category.

Of course, real life is often more complex than that. You may find a solution that meets all of your needs but is very difficult to work with. However, it may come in at a much lower price than the others, or even be free. In this common case, it is important to make sure that you are comparing similar systems. If system A and system B have equivalent functionality, but system B is a lot more fun to use, it wins the Utility check. However, you may want to keep system A in the mix because there are compelling features that are not in the primary criteria. In this case, score it in the lower mid-range for Utility and add a note to address the shortcomings in a later phase. This is common for open source deployments, where the low cost makes them very attractive, but you may need to allocate training time to the calculation used in the price negotiation.

Unlike the other assessment variables, Utility does not cleanly break down along technical and nontechnical lines. Any glaring technical drawbacks along the Utility variable will have been excluded already because they do not provide the Required features. This leaves the fuzzy middle ground. In some assessments, this will result in every vendor being scored in the mid-range for Utility, and your decisions will be made with other variables. In other assessments, you'll get to the Deep Dive phase, do trial installs and find out that some systems simply fail. Vendors who are trying to get into a new market niche frequently exaggerate their products' capabilities. If this results in them not being fit for your purposes, exclude them and move on. You can always reconsider them when they mature enough to meet your needs.

To get more independent data about the utility of the system, it can help to talk to actual users. See if the vendor will provide you with a list of reference accounts (people who, due to the vendor's involvement, are biased in favor of the vendor). Then build your own list of "discovered customers" by searching the Internet for companies discussing the technology in forums and mailing lists.

Testing Table—Utility

Technology—Research
   • What is the ratio of unresolved issues to total issues in the public issue tracking system? (10 min)
   • What percentage of dialog boxes seen in screenshots use the same UI layout? (10 min)

Technology—Hands On
   • How easy is it to reset your password? (5 min)
   • How easy is it to add a task/project/record? (10 min)

Nontechnical—Research
   • How long did each reference account take to get the system up and functioning? (30 min)
   • When pressed, what percentage of discovered customers complain about the vendor? (2 h)

Nontechnical—Hands On
   • How easy is it to discover which person in the vendor's company you need to talk to in the event of a business critical issue? (5 min)
   • How long does it take to get that person to respond to you via phone or e-mail? (5 min/48 h)

3.1.7 Testing Integrity

Because properly testing the integrity of a system requires access to the system at a level that you are unlikely to have at this point, you are limited to testing the integrity of the vendor and relying on third-party reports. One great source of integrity issues are public bug trackers. Check each vendor candidate against http://www.securityfocus.com/vulnerabilities/. Search for known exploits at http://www.exploit-db.com/search/. As you find potential concerns with the technology, search on the Common Vulnerabilities and Exposures (CVE) number for the issue and see how long it took between when the issue was reported and when it was corrected. Other internal integrity issues can be identified if the vendor makes it to the second round of testing.

Testing the personal integrity of a business can be tricky. In many ways, you'll never know if they're trustworthy or not until they do something that hurts you. However, there are two tests that can work. The first is to run legal searches against the name of the company and of each of the officers as well as that of the salesperson you're working with. Most lawsuits are public and, while you may not get many details, if a company that's only been around for a relatively short time has several lawsuits against it, it should be a red flag. The second is to ask your personal network. Don't bother asking the vendor for references, they're not going to give you bad ones. Instead, go to various networking groups or call other organizations in your industry and see what they say. You may hear "yeah, I worked with them and they were great," but if you hear "I don't want to speak ill of someone else, but I wouldn't work with them again," consider that a red flag.

Consider, though, that red flags differ by geographic region. For example, a negative opinion on the East coast of the United States may sound like "Don't use those guys, they suck." On the West coast, they may say "The product was good, but not quite good enough." In the upper Midwest, it could be expressed as "Their design choices were interesting." And in the South, you could simply not get an answer at

Testing Table—Integrity
Technology—Research
• What is the average time for the vendor to resolve reported problems in the system? (2 h)
• If the data has an identifiable characteristic, how many hits for leaked system data can you find on the Internet? (5 min)
Technology—Hands On
• How easily can you, as any account on the test system, change the data of any other account? (30 min)
• What information is logged when you change a data record? (15 min)
Nontechnical—Research
• How often has the vendor been sued by existing customers? (15 min)
• How many existing or former clients recommend doing business with the vendor? (30 min)
Nontechnical—Hands On
• When pressed on inaccuracies in the initial presentation, how does the vendor respond? (5 min)
• How does the vendor respond to reported concerns by current and former customers? (5 min)

all. If you are used to the communication style of your region, this shouldn't be a problem, but if you have recently moved, it might be good to have a native help you with translation.

3.1.8 Testing Authenticity

Authenticity checks may not apply in all situations. Mostly, this is reflected by country limits in legal requirements. In the United States, many firms that provide services to the Federal government are banned from using non-US encryption technologies. Most firms in the United States are prevented from doing business with specific countries that are deemed dangerous enough to warrant an embargo. So, in these cases, testing the authenticity of a system should be easy, but by that very token, such firms shouldn't make it this far into the analysis as they would not meet the Required feature of "being US based" or whatever may apply.

Instead, if you get to this point, you should consider issues of trust. This is similar to the OEM issue discussed in Possession/Control, but unlike that, the worry is not about the untrusted party taking control of your system. Instead, the concern is simply whether you can trust the work that the vendor did and whether their claim that they did the work is trustworthy. In most cases, this will be true, but just as students are spot-checked for plagiarism, you should do occasional checks that you're getting what you expect. Non-Western cultures appear to have looser concepts of intellectual property than do Western nations, and basing a critical business process on a technology that turns out to have been stolen can be catastrophic.

Verify that the technology that you are assessing is not black or gray market. Most gray market providers will let you know if you ask. Black marketers may not. So if, for example, you are purchasing a Cisco device from a new VAR vendor, it's worth the 2 minutes it would take to call Cisco and verify the vendor's legitimacy. If the vendor you are assessing provides the technology directly, ask where it comes from. Very few vendors build everything 100% in house. Most technology is based on other technology. A good vendor will tell you what their stack is built on. If they don't, and you grow concerned, you'll need to dig a little bit deeper. This is where LinkedIn and resume searches can be useful.

Few employees stay with an employer forever. When they leave, their resume and online job hunting profiles often list their previous firms. A simple web search on "resume [company name]" can turn up previous employees. A LinkedIn search on a company or a Google

Testing Table—Authenticity

Technology—Research
   · How prevalent are black market versions of the vendor's product? (15 min)
   · How tolerant is the vendor of gray market versions of the vendor's product? (5 min)

Technology—Hands On
   · How many LICENSE or README files exist on the demo system that the vendor did not report? (15 min)
   · How many copyright claims exist in metadata in the system? (15 min)

Nontechnical—Research
   · How many upstream technology partners does the vendor list on their home page? (5 min)
   · How many people on the Internet complain about theft by the vendor? (5 min)

Nontechnical—Hands On
   · How do former employees react to concerns about the vendor? (30 min)
   · How many complaints about ownership exist on public forums run by the vendor? (10 min)

search on "site:linkedin.com [company name]" will turn up lists of people. Just start calling and e-mailing, explaining your concerns, and asking why they left. If they're still very positive about the company, ask about the technology stacks. If they're negative or guarded about the company, see if you can find out why. That might reflect along another variable but should be tracked.

3.1.9 A Note on Adjusting Criteria

As you go through this process, it is common to discover that some of your initial criteria were incorrect or lacking. So, it's tempting to add items to your criteria list as you go. While there is nothing wrong with this, it can be dangerous to compare vendors and products against a sliding scale. So, as you adjust criteria, be sure to cycle back to the first ones assessed to make sure that everything is covered fairly. This is easily done if you track your findings in the matrix mentioned previously. If, however, you are using a different method, such as working off standardized forms that are passed out to team members for comparison, you may have to regenerate the forms and do a second cycle through this phase of analysis before you are ready to go on to the next.

PHASE 4

Scoring, Weighting, and Sorting

4.1 SCORING, WEIGHTING, AND SORTING

Now, it is time to score your vendors. You have assigned questions to each variable and gone through the process and answered all questions for all vendors. Now you need to average each variable's questions together and begin scoring them. While you can arrange the scale any way you prefer and do complex weighting, I find it works best to use a simple positively maximized linear scale and weight at the end. That sentence is horribly mathy, so let me elaborate with an example:

If you were analyzing a firewall vendor for Availability, you would have questions like:

Availability:

- How much sustained traffic can the vendor's product handle?

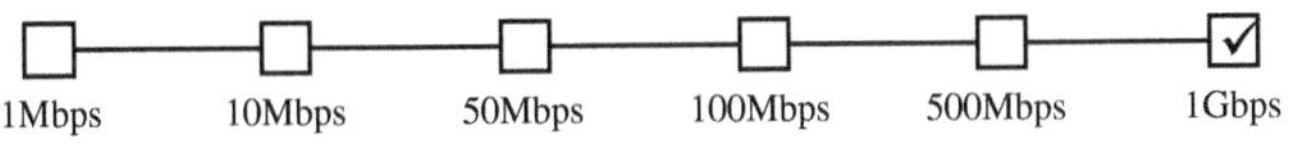

- How much peak traffic can the vendor's product handle?

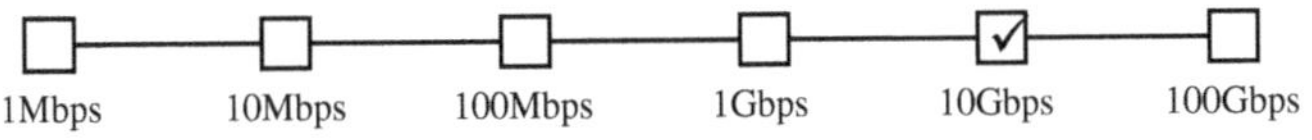

- How feasible is it to implement multiple devices and cluster them for redundancy?

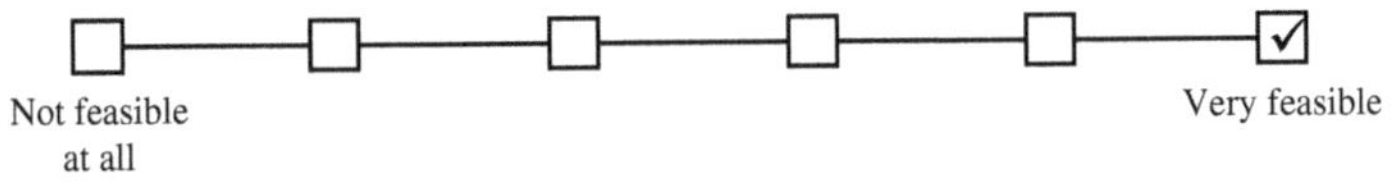

- How feasible is it to implement a "fail open"configuration so traffic passes in the event of failure?

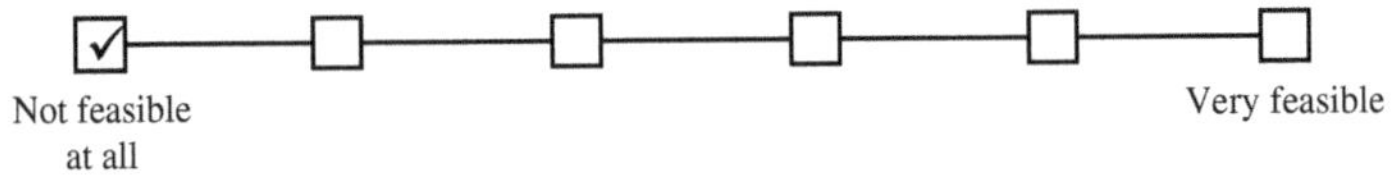

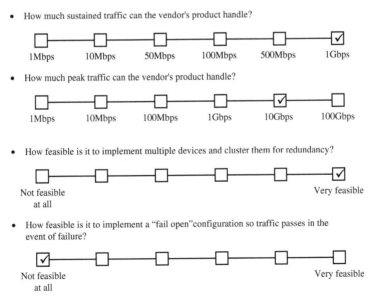

Even though the numerical scales appear nonlinear in this example, their metrics are, as you give the first position in each Likert item a value of one and the last one a value of six. Thus, they score as follows:

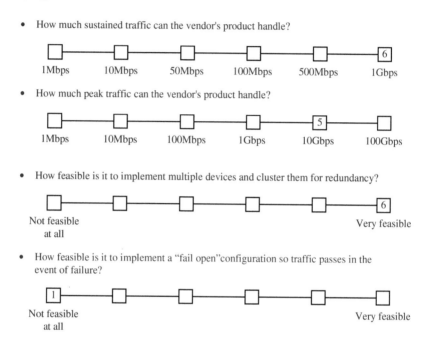

- How much sustained traffic can the vendor's product handle?

  1Mbps   10Mbps   50Mbps   100Mbps   500Mbps   1Gbps [6]

- How much peak traffic can the vendor's product handle?

  1Mbps   10Mbps   100Mbps   1Gbps   10Gbps [5]   100Gbps

- How feasible is it to implement multiple devices and cluster them for redundancy?

  Not feasible   Very feasible [6]
  at all

- How feasible is it to implement a "fail open"configuration so traffic passes in the event of failure?

  [1]
  Not feasible   Very feasible
  at all

So the averaged score for Availability is $(6 + 5 + 6 + 1)/4 = 5$. You'd then go through the process for each variable and wind up with a score list for each vendor. The score can then be normalized by dividing it by the total number of points available and expressing it as a percentage. This percentage gives you an estimate as to how well the option would compare to an idealized, nonexistent, option.

It must be stressed that this option is, in fact, nonexistent. You will never find a real vendor with a normalized score of 100%. In fact, if you do a good job of choosing your questions, you'll seldom see one in the 80–90%. Most of them will cluster around the average, as most questions will be answered as "sorta good" or "sorta bad," not "this is the best match to the feature that can possibly exist." Don't stress if you get several low scores for vendors you like. The importance is the relative difference between vendors, not whether they get an A+ or C− in the assessment process.

As an example, suppose you did this for firewalls and wound up with the following score lists. In these examples, the made-up firewalls are such that Augustus and Carinus firewalls are optimized for availability. This is, perhaps, because they are aimed at the ISP market. Balbinus focuses on confidentiality and perhaps targets the financial industry. Diocletian is different and focuses entirely on utility. Because it is completely internally designed, it lacks features that other firewalls have, but completely maxes out the authenticity check. Consider this one a late-to-market disruptive vendor.

	Augustus	Balbinus	Carinus	Diocletian
Availability	5	2	6	1
Possession/Control	3	4	1.5	4.5
Confidentiality	5.5	6	4	1
Utility	2	4.33	4	6
Integrity	4.5	2	2	1
Authenticity	3.33	2.5	4	6
Total	23.33	20.83	21.5	19.5
Normalized score (/36)	64.8%	57.9%	59.7%	54.2%

As you can see, they're rather similar, but Augustus edges out the three competitors.

However, this is an unweighted analysis. Suppose you were most concerned about Utility and decided that that variable was twice as important as the others and that you didn't care about availability as much, so it was worth half. The scoring would shift as follows:

	Augustus	Balbinus	Carinus	Diocletian
Availability (/2)	5/2	2/2	6/2	1/2
Possession/Control	3	4	1.5	4.5
Confidentiality	5.5	6	4	1
Utility ($\times 2$)	2×2	4.33×2	4×2	6×2
Integrity	4.5	2	2	1
Authenticity	3.33	2.5	4	6
Total	22.83	24.16	22.5	25
Normalized score (/39)	58.5%	61.9%	57.7%	64.1%

Suddenly, Diocletian is the winner and Augustus is in third place. This example may seem contrived, but in truth, there are several disruptive vendors in most vendorspace and it often does break down this way. Disruptive vendors tend to lack features and make a horrible showing on a straight analysis, but completely take over if your needs and their strengths align. Utility is a common area for this to happen, as most traditional vendors tend to build interfaces that feel very similar to one another and it takes a disruptive influence to shake things up and get one vendor to get noticed. Back when all firewalls were administered by the command line, Check Point was one of the first vendors to disrupt the market with a GUI. This won them a lot of business until a bunch of UTM vendors (Fortinet, Astar, Watchguard, etc.) copied that idea and Check Point no longer had a Utility advantage over some of its competitors.

As this book is being written, there is a similar shake-up occurring in the Log Management vendorspace. Traditional log management solutions have gathered logs together and allowed you to generate reports and look for outliers. However, companies such as Splunk, Boundary, and Loggly are changing the game by creating systems that give the user a search engine sort of interface. Other managed service vendors such as Solutionary and Alert Logic have products that may score lower on Utility but make up for them by filtering data through outsourced analysis teams. In effect, these tools are optimized to the teams, not the end user. In this sort of situation, additional Utility questions may be added to the list to cover such scenarios ... assuming that outsourcing log management was considered acceptable in your environment.

While you can be extremely detailed in how you choose to weight your variables, it is very important to weight them at the beginning of the process. Choosing weights during the final analysis is a common manipulation of this sort of process to get a preselected vendor on the short list. While you can certainly take this approach, you are effectively wasting your effort up to this point, as the advantage of the process is to help you learn new things about vendor ranking and possibly pick someone new. If you are checking someone else's work running through this process, a telltale sign of manipulation is to see strange weights. In most cases, weighting by powers of two or three should be sufficient to tilt the direction to a vendor you should consider. Weights larger or smaller than this indicate that someone is manipulating the process to get their vendor to win, that you have a variable you do not need, or that you have multiple concepts wrapped up into a single variable. In the last case, you should go back to the beginning and reconsider this entire phase with new variables.

4.1.1 Filtering Out Losers

The goal of the preceding phase was two-fold. First, it was designed as a second filter run focused on vendors that are unsuitable, whether for technical or business reasons. By this point, each vendor should be scored along six variables. Now, you need to determine how fast you want to go. The more vendors you filter out here, the fewer you have to consider down the road.

Conservatively, it is reasonable to aim at filtering out 20% of the vendors as no longer being worth consideration. When you select the top 20% of your list to be your "short list" vendors, you'd still have a pool of the remaining 60% in case your short list vendors fail the deep tests. You can also filter ruthlessly and look to get rid of the vast majority of the vendors, trying to cut your workspace by 75%. Everyone remaining would then be on the short list. This would, of course, mean that if you exclude all 25% during deep testing, you'd have to resort the bottom 75%.

The approach you take will depend on how quickly you have to make a decision and how flexible that decision needs to be. If you must select your first choice by the end of the week, you should filter out as many as you possibly can at this stage. If, however, this is a year-long project with a high cost of change (common in large enterprises and government), you should proceed conservatively and aim to be better able to justify your decision at the end of the process.

This is where your weighted scores come in handy. Simply line up all your vendors, pick your cutoff margin, and eliminate all the vendors that don't make the cut.

4.1.2 Selecting Winners

As the next phase is to take a deeper dive into specific solutions, the major goal here is to cut the list to a manageable number. This is going to depend on the complexity of the vendorspace that you are assessing. In general, the older a technology is, the simpler it is to use, understand, and assess. Technology that is new or that has a new way of blending older technologies is more complex and will take longer.

At the time of writing this book, technologies like firewalls and antivirus systems are relatively simple. Anti-malware and intrusion detection systems fall somewhere in the middle. And newer technologies such as "Big Data" analytics tools and automated intelligence appliances are highly complex.

While the precise number of candidates on the final short list is up to you, a good rule of thumb is no more than six for simple options and no less than three for complex ones. If you select more than six solutions, the Deeper Dive phase of testing will take longer than it is worth and if you select less than three, you might as well just pick your favorite and stop. Having a third option to compare your first and second choices against does wonders for helping you make less biased decisions.

That said, there's nothing necessarily wrong with stopping here and just going with your favorite. After all, you've done some basic due diligence and if you can trust the information that led you to this point, there's an argument to be made that you've done enough. However, if you choose to stop before you get to functional testing, it is very important to structure your initial deployment in such a way that it tests the system against your needs. This is often done as a "Paid Proof of Concept" (PPoC) in which you and the vendor agree on how you'll be testing the system with the agreement that if it passes the tests, you will purchase the system. This approach is often biased in favor of the vendor winning this PPoC process. However, this bias isn't that critical. As long as you are good at setting up the PPoC, you'll wind up with a system that meets your needs. All you lose out on by taking this approach is some negotiation power when it comes to pricing.

PHASE 5

Deep Testing

5.1 DEEP TESTING

When you get to the Deep-Testing phase, you should be down to three to six vendors. The goal here is strictly to assess how well they will meet your needs. You've done your research, watched videos, played with demos, and done whatever you needed to do to answer the basic filtering questions. Now it's time for them to prove what they can do.

Once again, it is important to keep time from running away from you, but it is extremely unlikely that you will be able to do deep functional testing for a vendor in a day or even two. The length of time will depend mostly on your time and dollar budgets. Larger organizations can take months to assess a vendor, while smaller organizations sometimes skip this step completely and just go with someone they know works. Any approach along this continuum is valid. However, to keep things relatively realistic, the rest of this section will assume that you have decided that a week is sufficient time to assess each vendor and that a week is also sufficient time to set up the test itself.

These numbers were chosen because, for most technologies that aren't horribly complex, a week is enough time to find flaws that will derail the actual use of the technology but not so long that you wind up getting lost in the details. These numbers will not be sufficient for technologies that require a long tuning period, such as Data Loss Prevention (DLP) or network white-listing technologies. However, those vendors are not likely to allow you to do free testing as the functional test itself would provide you with enough value to indicate it might make good economic sense to simply use that data to fix your issues and not purchase the product.

5.2 FAIR VERSUS UNFAIR TESTING

It is important to keep in mind that you are looking for a solution to a problem, not for a way to cheat the vendor. As soon as you lose sight of this, you risk crossing the line into unfair testing. A solution will only work as long as both you and your eventual vendor partner work together on it. Sadly, it is common in IT for vendors and customers to take a somewhat adversarial approach toward one another. This can result in lower pricing, but it also often results in lower reliability. Fundamentally, no technology is perfect and what makes the difference between a bug being annoying and catastrophic is often the vendor's response. If you take advantage of the vendor in this phase to build up an artificial advantage for future negotiation, the chances of your getting priority help when you need it will be extremely low.

A fair test is one in which you have a clear set of criteria and all vendors on the short list understand and agree their products match the criteria. In edge cases, you have identified areas in which the technologies do not fit and have identified a set of workarounds for those issues. At the end, you wind up with a plan for each vendor that can be implemented relatively quickly and, when done, all vendors will be on fairly equal footing.

Unfair tests are those you go into wanting one vendor to win or wanting to abuse the process to get useful data without making a purchase. You can certainly enter into a test with a favorite, but as this is a data-driven process, you should feel obligated to select the vendor with the best data. To do otherwise will harm everyone involved. The vendors against whom the test is tilted will be less likely to work with you in the future should you need them. This unwillingness may even follow you to a new job, as this is part of a sales process and sales are relationship-based. Also, the vendor that wins a tilted test is less likely to work with you on features or price, as they know they were selected even though they weren't the best candidate.

On the vendor side, a mark of an unfair test is that they require you to sign a Nondisclosure Agreement (NDA) prior to testing. While there is nothing wrong with NDAs, some NDAs prevent you from sharing the results of your testing with others. While these provisions are often added as a concern that unfair testing on your part could damage their chances with other clients, they are a fundamental mark of mistrust. If the vendor is unwilling to negotiate on the NDA, it may be worth considering replacing them with a vendor who is more willing to work with you.

A positive side of NDAs, however, is that it can protect the vendor's use of your data during the test. If at all possible, use nonproduction fabricated data during this assessment process. If it is not possible, pursue an NDA, but for your own protection, not the vendor's.

5.3 IDENTIFYING NEEDS

For this phase of the assessment, go back to your feature list and review the Required and Would Be Nice items. Ask yourself why those matter. Think of scenarios in which each feature would be used. Put an estimate on how much time it would take to test each scenario and how critical the scenario is to your business.

Consider these scenarios for common vendorspaces. However, as mentioned previously, be very careful to avoid turning example lists like this into generalized lists to use for multiple assessments. The more general you get, the less well tuned your final selection will be to your specific needs.

The flip side of this approach is that your scenarios will be very specific to your needs. Take these following tables as examples. If you are not actively seeking a solution in one of these areas, the scenarios selected will not be very useful (or possibly intelligible) to you. However, if you are, they enable you to rapidly focus on your precise needs and not waste time digging through generalities.

Next Generation Firewall/Unified Threat Management		
Stateful tracking of connections is Required. Can you easily route complex connections such as FTP or encrypted antimalware message routing through the firewall?	0.5 h	Critical
The ability to block and allow traffic based on IP address and protocol is Required. Can you set up a rule to allow HTTP traffic, regardless of port to Server A but still have access to Server B blocked by default?	0.5 h	Critical
Support for VLAN tagging is Required. Secure support Would Be Nice. Can you create multiple VLANs for security zones and have traffic with manually manipulated VLAN tags logged and dropped?	1 h	Critical
Support for Microsoft's Active Directory Would Be Nice. Can you connect the device to the domain controller and have it automatically track and report connections by user instead of IP?	4 h	Noncritical
Two physical ports is Required but eight Would Be Nice. Once networks are connected to the appropriate ports, is it possible to bypass the rules limited traffic?	1 h	Critical

Backups		
The ability to back up Windows and Linux hosts is Required. Can you perform a backup for each operating system in use?	4 h	Critical
Restore of critical systems within 30 min is Required. Verify that this is possible by taking a backup of each critical system and performing a restore into a test network.	12 h	Critical
The ability to do bare metal restores Would Be Nice. How difficult is this to do?	1 h	Noncritical
The ability to browse backup archives and extract key files without performing a full restore Would Be Nice. Is this capability available?	2 h	Noncritical

Antimalware		
The ability to block malware based on signature is Required. Does the system properly detect and block the EICAR test file?	0.5 h	Critical
The ability to block malware based on behavior is Required. Does an isolated system allow the latest versions of the following malware to run? Zeus, FakeAV, Sality, PGPcoder, and Rimecud	8 h	Critical
On demand reporting is Required. Can you easily generate a report showing you the IP address, username, and operating system of an infected system that shows the type and time of infection?	1 h	Critical
Control over potentially malicious applications Would Be Nice. Can you configure the system to detect and block things like the Google Toolbar, WeatherBug, and WinZip?	2 h	Noncritical
Scheduled reporting Would Be Nice. Can you take the report you ran previously and set it to run every night and be sent to the appropriate personnel?	1 h	Noncritical
Integration with a host-based firewall Would Be Nice. Can you configure network traffic at a host-level and control what traffic can flow to and through your endpoints?	4 h	Noncritical
Integration with the existing log management system Would Be Nice. Can you redirect the logs and/or alerts so there is a streamlined reporting flow?	8 h	Noncritical

Web Application Firewall		
The ability to protect PHP sites running on Apache is Required. Does the system have native support for this language and platform to detect custom targeted attacks?	4 h	Critical
The ability to block SQL injection attacks is Required. Does the system detect and block attacks generated by SQL InjectMe and SQLMap?	8 h	Critical
The ability to block Cross Site Scripting attacks is Required. Does the system detect and block attacks from Arachni and Skipfish?	2/16 h[*]	Critical
Multisite support is Required. Can you configure the system to protect two different sites with two different site profiles?	4 h	Critical
The ability of the multisite implementation to allow for specific administrators affiliated with each site Would Be Nice. Can you configure individual administrators that do not have access to one another's configuration areas?	2 h	Noncritical
Specific awareness of the MySQL database system Would Be Nice. Does the firewall detect and block MySQL-specific metadata attacks?	4 h	Noncritical
The ability to use the system as a virtual patching layer Would Be Nice. Does the vendor provide a vulnerability feed that can be matched to your system and activated as needed?	4 h	Noncritical

[*] *Cross Site Scripting attacks can take quite a while to run but does not require human inspection during that time.*

E-mail Server or Services		
The ability to communicate via SMTP, POP, and IMAP is required. Can Outlook and Thunderbird clients connect to the e-mail server and send e-mail to one another?	8 h	Critical
The support for antispam protocols such as SPF and DKIM are Required. Once the system is configured to support them, can they be bypassed via direct telnet/netcat testing of the SMTP interface?	4 h	Critical
The ability for users to proxy into one another's accounts without sharing passwords with one another is Required. Can this be done?	2 h	Critical
Support of mailing lists Would Be Nice. Can you create a list for internal users to communicate with one another? Can this list be protected from access by outside entities? Is there a secure way to create a list for people external to the system to use?	4 h	Noncritical
Support for e-mail archives Would Be Nice. Can all e-mail be archived on the system? Does it cause storage bloat? Does it slow down system processing?	2 h	Noncritical
Integration with the phone system Would Be Nice. Can you automatically e-mail voice mail messages? Can you trigger a phone call by clicking a link within an e-mail message?	4 h	Noncritical
The ability to use the system as a virtual patching layer Would Be Nice. Does the vendor provide a vulnerability feed that can be matched to your system and activated as needed?	4 h	Noncritical

Next, review all the requirements for an installation or deployment. Resolve each dependency so when it's time to start your assessment, you don't lose any time to provisioning new servers, IP addresses, or waiting for other people to have time. Once you have identified the assessment window for a vendor, you have to be able to hit it as hard and as fast as you can. This means that during your set up time, you have to build these scenario lists, ready all the hardware, download all the software, and send out all the calendar appointments you think you'll need to get opinions from others. Then, put an estimate what each install will take and cut that out of the time available for postinstall testing.

To help you along, consider this list of common needs when deploying new technology:

- IP reservations—internal and external
- Server availability—physical or virtual
- Backup agents/configuration
- Endpoint software installation
- "Feeds" to other systems, such as log detail or e-mail
- "Feeds" from other systems, such as log aggregation or data for reporting
- List of external systems to which the technology must connect and their protocols
- Firewall rules and test scripts to support this list
- List of users and databases that must be used
- List of DNS changes that must be made to activate the test system.

Since some systems will be easier to install than others, you will have to cut different amounts of time out of testing windows for each vendor. If, for example, one vendor deploys its own version of SQL Server Express, you may have as little as one hour to install, as you just run the executable and let it go. If, however, another vendor has a virtual appliance that must be configured, another appliance that manages the first and must connect into a data warehouse for disk storage, that install may chew up two entire days. This means that you'd have 39 hours of testing for the first vendor but only 24 hours for the second. This will greatly affect the set of scenarios that you can run.

You are looking for a set of scenarios that test most of the features you need within the available time. If it takes you 24 hours to test one scenario, 48 hours to test another, and 12 hours each to test each of six others, you'd not have enough time in a week to test them all. Figure out which set of scenarios best fits your needs for the candidate with the minimal window. If that does not give you sufficient testing time, consider extending the windows so all vendors may be fairly assessed. You may do this in one of two ways.

First, simply extending the time for each vendor may be good enough. If you have originally allocated one week per vendor, consider pushing to a week and a half.

However, to be completely fair, you may wish to separate the install/deployment testing from the "in use" testing. This is often a better use of time, as in one week; you might get all of your technologies installed (assuming they do not conflict with one another). Then, you'd have one week to test each vendor. This approach also lends itself to scheduling people as a problem in the deployment phase is less likely to push the future testing appointments into the future. The drawback to this approach, though, is that lengthy installs may not reflect as poorly on the vendor as you'd prefer. The priority of install issues will depend in part on how often you'll be doing the installs. If you'll only install a solution once, it may not be a concern, but if you have to install one at each of 20 different offices and again for disaster recovery concerns, and the update process is effectively a reinstall, you might want to weight install issues extremely high.

Then, as you crunch through scenarios, you score in a similar way as you did in the initial process. However, since you will likely be doing this testing in a team environment, the totals at the end will have to be added up and then averaged. This may mean giving your team some scoring sheets or, if you wish to go high-tech, build a little survey system to collect the data. There are plenty online systems that you can use, though the most common are Google Docs and Survey Monkey. If you wish to use this functionality more than once, it may be worthwhile to run a quick vendor assessment against in the IT Survey Space.

Next, using the same variables as before, dive into each scenario, and score the vendors.

5.3.1 Deep-Testing Availability
Availability testing a real-world scenario can come in many flavors. If the technology is user-facing, once your users use it, ask them what they would do if it became unavailable. Odds are they'd initially respond with plans to go back to whatever they're using today. If this is a replacement technology, be sure to clarify that what's available

today would not be available. Once they've come up plans, you can ask them questions like:

- How painful would it be to be without this solution?

Not painful   Extremely
at all   painful

- How long would it take to recover from losing this solution?

2–5 days   1–2 days   8–24h   4–8h   1–4h   0–1h

If the solution is not user-facing, you can pull in metrics from other systems. The quantity and accuracy of these metrics will depend on how tightly integrated the technology will be. In this situation, it is often easier to just collect the raw data on all vendors and then develop your scales at the end of the process. Just be careful to calibrate the scales so they are fair to everyone. Good questions to ask here include:

- How much sustained bandwidth did the system process before it became unresponsive?
- How much peak bandwidth did the system process before it became unresponsive?
- How much disk I/O did the system handle before it became unresponsive?

Once you have this information from each of your vendors, you should be able to assign Likert-style bins to each question to streamline the data into your final analysis process.

Common availability scenarios:

- After the system is fully configured, unplug it during operation to determine how it responds to power interruption. Metrics to consider include time to initial recovery (when the system is usable) and time to full recovery (once all processes and users are caught up). If the system comes with technology to help manage this risk, also consider the types of alerts you get prior to the outage, such as when a UPS activates and begins the countdown to true shutdown.
- Test network availability by launching DDoS tools against the system during operation. Consider tools such as HULK, HOIC, and LOIC. Look to see if processes complete more slowly or if they are

simply interrupted via default timeouts. See if the timeout values can be adjusted. Perhaps most importantly, look for situations under which the user is notified that the process completed successfully, but any changes were not actually written to disk or sent to a receiving system.

- Test authentication availability by launching password brute-forcing tools against the system during operation. Consider tools such as Cain and Abel, John The Ripper, Ophcrack, Brutus, and THC Hydra. Look for account lockouts and whether those counts are configurable. If the accounts should lock out and do not, that should be considered a negative. If the accounts do lockout, you may wish to measure the ease with which a sufficiently-privileged user can reset the lock.

5.3.2 Deep-Testing Possession/Control

Testing this variable can seriously break things, it may be best to hold this for last. This is where you test your assumptions from your initial research. As you will be installing systems, find out what a reasonably skilled person can do with control over the system. Once you've gathered all the data you can, turn control of the system over to someone else in your organization. Give them tasks to perform and time them. In general, this test will likely reverse correlate with the Utility data, as the easier a system is to use, the easier it will be to take over if someone gets possession of it.

You can also test for remote control capabilities by conducting an active port scan with NMAP against the system and for default username and password combinations by using a password brute-forcing tool like THC Hydra. Be aware that these may lock you out of the system if they are detected as attacks. Also, be aware that they will not give you a high level of certainty that the system is "safe." Their purpose is to let you know if they are susceptible to attack.

Common possession/control scenarios:

- Can a user create another user with equal or lower privileges so that that user can make system changes or alter financial data? If so, is there a way to do this such that no other individuals are notified? The concern here is whether or not a rogue user can use the system to embezzle money or steal information in a way that is not directly traceable to them.

- If an individual is given physical control of the system, how long does it take them to access sensitive data? Because physical access is a "game over" situation for many uses, this is a good way to determine how much physical control the system will require to stay secure.
- If an individual were to gain physical control of the system, how susceptible would the system be to later use attacks? This can be tested by adding keyloggers or password harvesters to the system. In this scenario, the system is assumed to be reasonably secure with respect to direct access, so an attacker would plant technology in place to gather the data needed to unlock aspects of the system for a subsequent physical attack.

5.3.3 Deep-Testing Confidentiality

Now that you have a full system to play with, you get to try to break in to it. First, look at the system-level. If there are databases involved, attempt to access them outside of the system. This may be via the network or via local disk browsing. A system with a high confidentiality threshold will make this difficult, but there are a great many systems that do not. Another area of confidentiality failure can include encryption failure. This is harder for a nonexpert to test, but if you can, try to identify the primary encryption key, then use system search utilities to see if it exists anywhere in temporary storage or RAM. Forensics tools can be very useful here. Needless to say, if the security of the system is going to be business-critical, it may be wise to enlist the services of an expert. My own expert weighs in on this topic in the last section of this chapter.

Next, look at the application level. See if one user can access another user's data. This may be by manipulating session information in a web application or by accessing different paths in a thick-client. If you have the skill, see what running a memory debugger can do. The details of that level of assessment is beyond the scope of this book, but if you are interested, check out the techniques discussed in *Exploiting Online Games* by Greg Hogland and Gary McGraw (Addison-Wesley, 2007) to learn how to use the tools properly.

At this level, you can also run a game among your team members. Create an account with some deliberately crafted data in it. It's best to use a pairwise system, where you create a data element with two unique random phrases, such as "cai1salmooboohD7ae" and "Aij8meew3nai4ERi." Give your team the first phrase and ask them to find the second in any way they can. If they return the second phrase properly, find out how they did it and use that information to adjust the score. Then reward them with a $100 gift card. One hundred dollars, when compared to the cost of purchasing an enterprise system is a mere pittance, but it is great for getting the team to hit a system hard.

If you find a failure here, it may not necessarily be horrible. It just means that you have to protect access at a different level. This may require additional technology or a different operations plan but should certainly be possible. The complexity and expense of this sort of solution should be considered. If a vendor got to this point, it is not wise to exclude them entirely based on a single failure.

Common confidentiality scenarios:

- Given a list of sensitive data elements on the system, how many items can a team of testers get in 10 minutes? In 20 minutes? In an hour?
- Assume the primary administrator on the system has been killed in a freak gardening accident. How quickly can a new administrator get into the system to deliver critical data to the business?
- If the system uses encryption, assume the encryption key is lost. Is it possible to do a reset with vendor assistance? If so, how difficult is it to do and is the process such that if someone were to gain access to the vendor systems, your data would be at risk?

5.3.4 Deep-Testing Utility

As with the surface-level testing, this may be the most critical variable to test in Deep Testing. If your people reject a system for being too hard to use, it's not going to be used whether you buy it or not. Conduct this test as before but spread the scoring across the team. Devise a list of common tasks that for which your people will have to use the system and have them do the tasks while assessing the ease of doing it.

If you have the time, consider doing two batches of users, one that uses the system after having been trained on it and that uses the system without that advantage. In certain cases with particularly complex systems, trained users may find a particularly difficult system easier to use. As with Confidentiality, a Utility failure is not necessarily terrible. If you can bypass utility issues through training, you just need to include the cost of that training into your total estimate for final negotiation.

Common utility scenarios:

- How easily can a user be added to the system? How easily can they be removed?
- Can users reset their own passwords? If not, how easy is it for the administrator to do so?
- How easily can the technology be migrated to a new operating system?
- How easily can the system be backed up? How easily can it be restored?
- How easily can the system be integrated with your log management system?
- How quickly can an alert be traced within the system?

5.3.5 Deep-Testing Integrity

As mentioned previously, this is the time when you can truly dig in and test Integrity. This is a particularly interesting variable to test in a deep assessment. "Integrity" can refer to the integrity of the data in the system or the integrity of the system itself. Basically, what you care about here is whether your data and expectations remain unaltered from the time you start to when you need it again. For data, it's easy. Just test the same way you do with Confidentiality but go one step further. If you can read the data, can you change it? In some cases, you may be able to change the data without reading it, but unless you're a security expert with skill in blind injection, it's probably too complex of a test for this sort of rapid approach.

When testing the integrity of the system itself, you need to test stability. If you break something, will it fail cleanly? If you are able to identify the various components of the system, create a failure in each one to see how the system behaves. There are some systems that use transaction logging to replay faulty transactions but others that will lose or corrupt data in such situations.

Common integrity scenarios (often best combined with other variable tests):

- When doing the unplug test mentioned earlier, is any data corrupted? Is the system state clean?
- When doing the DDoS test mentioned earlier, is there risk of a process completing partially and not being rolled back if unsuccessful?

- How does the system behave when incorrect values are entered in configuration files or registry fields? How does it behave when "illegal" (nonsensical) values are entered?
- Can these configuration areas be altered by a user without the logically appropriate privileges to effectively take over a system?
- Deliberately fill the disk as the system is used and determine how the system responds once the disk is full.

5.3.6 Deep-Testing Authenticity

Most of your work for checking Authenticity will have been done in the first round. Here, you just have to confirm your suspicions. Most vendors that play nicely include the licenses of their third-party technology somewhere in the system. This is often in the click-agreements that you must agree to when you do the initial install. For other systems, you can search the system for files that indicate the use of ancillary technologies. What you're looking for is evidence that the vendor may not have been entirely truthful as to where their technology came from. It's up to you to decide how big a deal this is, but bear in mind that if a vendor doesn't understand how their own technology works, they will likely be unable to support you the way you need.

Common authenticity scenarios:

- Do a search at the operating system-level for the following terms, read each file, and track the owner of each piece of intellectual property: LICENSE, README, GPL, Apache, BSD, Public Domain, Copyright, Version. Does this list match that the vendor provided for you earlier?
- Configure Wireshark to act as a proxy or to listen to mirrored packets off the technology's gateway. Collect data for two weeks, and then check the outbound packets to see their destinations. Compare these destinations to the GeoIP database and make sure that the countries to which data is intended are those that you expect.

5.3.7 Cryptography Advice from Anthony J. Stieber

Because cryptography analysis can be something of a different problem, Anthony has kindly agreed to offer a bit of advice for testing cryptography within this paradigm.

Cryptography Evaluation

This book's process also works for cryptography. A thorough crypto-graphic evaluation process would require a book of its own; however, a Lean/Agile approach can help avoid the worst issues. But since a crypto system is only as strong as its weakest link, the assigned weights often need to be similar.

Cryptography, or "crypto," is more than just confidentiality by encryption. Each of cryptography's several components can be positively and negatively affected by each Parkerian Hexad variable.

See below under each Parkerian Hexad variable for descriptions of crypto system components. A deeper evaluation would also compare each crypto system component with all of the Parkerian Hexad variables.

Availability

Attackers, especially insiders, could turn off or down-grade the cryptogra-phy. Some crypto systems automatically and invisibly disable or degrade crypto to maintain throughput or compatibility. Backward compatibility is backward vulnerability.

- Is the crypto mandatory and always-on?
- Who or what can enable, disable, or degrade the crypto?
- How is enabled, disabled, or degraded crypto detected, logged, and alerted?
- How is crypto performance measured, can it perform adequately under load?

Possession/Control

If vendors generate the keys, then it's not your crypto, it's their crypto. Cryptographic keys **must** be secret, unpredictable, and random, or derived from other properly generated keys. Follow a cryptographic key life cycle:

- Who, what, when, where, and how were the cryptographic keys generated?
- When do cryptographic keys expire?
- How and when are they destroyed?
- Are hardware (HSM) enforced mandatory controls available?

Confidentiality

Kerckhoffs's principle: "A cryptosystem should be secure even if every-thing about the system, except the key, is public knowledge."

Vendors can claim secrecy of anything, but keys don't have a firm knowledge of industry cryptographic standards and don't know what they are doing. Start with the strongest cryptography available for your data's life span because reencrypting data can't protect data that's already been compromised. Encryption can't keep all cryptographic keys secret. Somewhere there must be at least one secret that must not be encrypted so it can decrypt data and other keys.

- What cryptographic requirements, standards, and regulations apply to your environment?
- Is the confidentiality strength life span as long or longer than the life span of your data?
- Are published, standard, and known secure cryptographic components used?
- Who knows the last cryptographic secret, and how is it protected and managed?

Utility
Unusable crypto systems aren't used and aren't secure.

- Is data recovery easy and secure?
- Are recurring tasks easy?
- Are critical but infrequent tasks easy enough?
- Are critical mistakes difficult to do?

Transparent encryption may also be transparent to the attacker.

Integrity
Confidentiality without integrity is untrustworthy. A single bit error in a cryptographic system can propagate into the loss of all encrypted data. A nonpropagating single bit error can invert a value: make a debit into a credit, an allergy into a prescription, or turn off security entirely.

- Is there a crypto integrity check for accidental or deliberate data errors?
- Is the integrity strength life span as long or longer than the life span of your data?

Authenticity
Both vendors and users can be weak points.

- How is the crypto system protected before delivery?
- Is the vendor's supply chain and distribution path authenticated and integrity checked?
- Is the crypto system itself authenticated and integrity checked?
- Is user authentication as strong as the other security?
- Is multiparty control available to deter insider attacks?

Quick References
- Kerckhoffs's   principle: https://en.wikipedia.org/wiki/Kerckhoffs%27s_principle
- US NIST SP800-131A Cryptographic Algorithms and Key Lengths: http://csrc.nist.gov/publications/PubsSPs.html

- NSA Suite B (emerging standard): https://en.wikipedia.org/wiki/NSA_Suite_B_Cryptography

Random Number Generators
- US NIST SP800-90A Random Bit Generators
- US NISTDual_ECDRBG (insecure)

Ciphers
- AES
- 3TDES (Three Key Triple DES) secure if used correctly
- RC4,2TDES (Two Key Triple DES) (insecure)

Cipher Block Modes of Operation
- CBC and CTR—separate integrity checks required
- XTS—data at rest only
- GCM and CCM—128 bit tags required
- ECB (insecure)

Public Key Cryptography
- RSA-2048
- DSA-2048
- Diffie-Hellman (DH) 2048 (requires authenticity check via RSA, DSA, or HMAC)
- RSA/DSA/DH-1024 (insecure)

Hash Functions
- SHA-256 and higher
- SHA-3-256 and higher
- HMAC
- MD5, SHA-1 (insecure)

Adjusting Needs

6.1 ADJUSTING NEEDS

As at the end of the first round of live testing, it is common to find that this process uncovered additional needs that you didn't know you had. If the needs are at a fairly high level, such as finding out that availability is much more important than you had thought, simply adjust the weighting of the more important variables to account for this. Then check your first run and make sure that the vendors that made it onto the short list are still the right ones. You may have to go back and do some more deep tests to make sure.

If your situation is more complex, you will probably need to adjust your scenarios and revisit previously tested systems. This may require increasing your testing time for all deep-tested vendors and adding new vendors to the list. If so, this is the point where you can throw the time-bound testing out the window as, at this point, it's pretty hard to get value from that sort of restricted fairness.

If you were using scoresheets, you may need to update the scenarios and run your people through another round of limited testing. If you were using surveys, be careful that the update process doesn't purge your previous data. It may be best to just create a new survey and combine the results later.

In the end, you should be able to look at your data and score it the same way you did in round one. Once scored, everyone on the team should be able to look at the resulting score and agree that it's fair. Make sure this is true before proceeding. If any member of the team disagrees with the resulting score, go back to through the data and identify where the discrepancy came from. Avoid the lure of adjusting the weights to make the results turn out the way you want. Instead, if anything needs to be adjusted, have a frank discussion about what was missed and why. If the team agrees that it is important enough to go through a third round of Deep Testing, go the third round. If it is not, it is best to let the results stand as is. To do otherwise is to wind up with a solution that does not meet your needs.

Success at this point is as much social and political as it is technological. If, for example, most of the team prefers Vendor A but the operations manager prefers Vendor B and the selected tool is critical to that team, the issues had better be worked out before anything is purchased and implemented. Otherwise you risk investing a lot of money and time into a solution that could be passive—aggressively killed after implementation.

Examples of situations in which items may be missed include:

- You are assessing a disk encryption technology on your existing hardware, but at the same time, the corporate contracts team is exploring replacing laptops with Android tablet devices. This should shift the project to testing encryption on another operating system.
- You are assessing a new organization-wide printer refresh, but management is exploring document imaging. This would require a complete pivot of the project, as there could be substantial reduction in the features needed on any new printers.
- You are assessing a new document management system to streamline processes for Human Resources (HR) but had forgotten to include a member of the recruitment team in the process, relying instead on the opinions of the HR Director. Because that person will not be using the system, your tests of Utility were incomplete and must be redone.
- You are assessing accounting systems based on your current needs but have forgotten to include the needs of a recent acquisition who bills in advance of services rendered as opposed to after. This would require your accounting system to handle both modes of operation and, more importantly, prevent double-billing as a result of human error from individuals confused between the two systems.

6.1.1 Selecting and Ranking the Final List

Unlike the filtering phase of the first round of analysis, this should be a very straightforward process. The variables are already weighted, so it's a matter of a bit of averaging, multiplying by the weights, and coming up with a final ranking of vendors. Then, it's time to talk to the first vendor on the list and go into discussions about production use and price negotiation.

Before we get to that point, though, here's a quick summary of what this stage of analysis should look like. In this example, the team has decided that, to protect client data, Confidentiality is a very important variable but due to government regulations Authenticity is twice as important as that. Utility falls somewhere between the two, as without regulatory approval, the entire project is dead, but the business could survive a single breach. However, without the acceptance of the internal operations team, the project is unlikely to succeed. Last, because the system is internal-only, Availability is less of a concern. Thus, they are weighted as seen below.

	Nicander	Praxilla	Sotades	Tyrtaeus
Availability (/2)	5.5/2	3.33/2	6/2	4.25/2
Possession/Control	3	4.5	5.125	4.5
Confidentiality ($\times 2$)	5.5×2	6×2	4×2	5.25×2
Utility ($\times 3$)	6×3	5.5×3	4.33×3	6×3
Integrity	4.5	5	4.66	3.5
Authenticity (/4)	6/4	3.5/4	4.5/4	6/4
Total	40.75	40.54	34.9	40.125
Normalized score (/46.5)	87.6%	87.2%	75.1%	86.3%

So, the winner is Nicander, followed closely by Praxilla and Tyrtaeus. Sotades comes in last and will likely not be considered unless the negotiation process fails spectacularly three times in a row.

Negotiating Price

7.1 NEGOTIATING PRICE

7.1.1 Project Management

As this assessment process is optimized for time, not for full coverage, there will always be items that remain unknown. However, if you did the deeper dive portion of the assessment, you will have a working system, if only in a test laboratory. In most cases, it is wise to reimplement the solution instead of simply moving the POC into production. This gives you a clean install that you can do having learned from the first time, but more importantly, there is no risk of data or configuration leakage that would affect production. This is especially true if you have turned the reins over to others to try to break the system while assessing it.

As you plan your final deployment, sit down with the entire team and run through a tabletop exercise to gather what everyone has learned. As before, use a time-based approach but instead of using a timer, use a calendar. Every piece of the initial deployment should be able to be mapped to a specific day and person. This is not a book on resource management, so feel free to use whatever project management methodology you prefer. Personally, I like to use Kanban, as it optimizes for data collection and work flow, albeit sometimes at the cost of certainty. More traditional environments will probably be more comfortable with Waterfall approaches and their Gantt chart focus. This approach optimizes for schedule certainty but requires more active management and so consumes more resources to enact.

Regardless of the management process chosen, it is likely that the project will break down into phases. Commonly, people approach phases from a feature perspective, but this can be risky. If you plan to implement specific features at specific times to meet business needs, a single delay will have cascading effects and can derail the entire project, causing you to miss multiple goals. What works better is to look at the project plan from a knowledge perspective. By this point, you know what you need to do a basic deployment. After all, you have already done one with this particular technology. However, there may be areas of uncertainty around specific elements of tuning, how to hook the technology into other areas of the business and how to interface with the vendor postsales.

These areas of uncertainty are "assessment gaps" and the goal of the tabletop exercise is to capture, as best you can, what you still do not know. This is often done by walking through the timeline of deployment and filling in the days that people will do specific tasks. If anyone claims that they can't do a task, find out if it is because they lack the knowledge or because they are overbooked. If they are overbooked, the team (or management) must come to agreement as to priorities. If they lack the knowledge, you need to categorize the gap.

What typically happens is that these assessment gaps come in three flavors. The first are questions that are easily answered by just asking someone, checking a knowledgebase article or reading documentation. The second are questions that are easily answered but take some time to do, as data must be gathered from other people or other systems. The third are questions that are not immediately answerable as they are dependent on the knowledge coming from the first two.

The first category of gaps is easily filled during the initial deployment by simply adding the time to the deployment plan. The second category typically falls into a "Phase 2—Tuning" category and deserves a second calendar of tasks that are to be executed once enough time has gone through to collect the day. However, if you are doing this, it is imperative to add items into "Phase 1—Deployment" that trigger the data collection process so it's ready for Phase 2 when you are. The third category is best handled with a simple list that is revisited in a Phase 3 kickoff whose purpose is to filter as many of these questions into category 1 or 2 so you can define Phases 3 and 4 of the deployment.

This means that Phases 1 and 2 will be tracked in calendar form, and Phases 3 and 4 will appear as a list. An example project may look like this:

M	T	W	T	F	S	S
2	3	4	5	6	7	8
	Provision server	Connect to DB	Load data into DB	Internal testing	Draft Phase 2 gap list	
9	10	11	12	13	14	15
	Deploy to test group	Train test group	Group testing	Group testing	Verify Phase 2 data	
16	17	18	19	20	21	22
	Address test concerns	Address test concerns	Address test concerns	Slack day	Deploy to production	Protection testing
23	24	25	26	27	28	29
	Production testing					
	Changeover slack day	Interviews	*Review gap data*	*Review gap data*	*Review gap data*	
30	31					
	Draft future phase plan					

Items for future phases:

- Database integration with backup software takes too long. Find a way to reduce this.
- Documentation insufficient for Services group. Revise.
- Nightly scheduled tasks collide with those for billing system. Reschedule.
- Implement redundancy services for system.
- WAIT   Test functionality with Windows 8
- WAIT—Test functionality with SQL Server 2015 prerelease.

Here, Phase 2 tasks are in italics and aim to simply identify tasks for future phases. Some of these tasks you know cannot get done in the next cycle, so you tag them with "WAIT". This way, they don't get lost, but you also don't feel overwhelmed by a massive list of TODO items.

Eventually, you will reach a point where the list of gaps are more easily answered or are coming in more slowly than they are being removed from the list. At this point, you can consider yourself fully operational with regard to the technology. For some technologies, this can take mere days. For others, it can take months. This will often depend on the complexity of the system but also on the average workload of your team.

Now, this does, of course, assume that none of the assessment gaps are critical.

"Critical" assessment gaps are those that, if the learned knowledge comes back in a certain way, it could kill the entire project. These are very rare. After all, if you did your due diligence in following the assessment process, most of the critical pieces should have already been identified as either working properly or having acceptable workarounds. However, there are always exceptions. If there is an element of uncertainty that has a reasonable chance of resolving in a way that kills the project, and there is no workaround available, it must be considered a critical gap.

If, in your initial process, you identify some of these critical gaps, you must document them and use them in negotiating price. Typical gaps include the following:

- The vendor promised that an item of functionality would be available by the next revision, but it is not available in the version you are testing. You can help to close this gap by looking at an alpha or beta version of the next revision.
- The vendor promised that the product will work with the new version of the operating system that is expected but not yet available. You can help close this gap by working measurable deliverables into the contract such as "three months after the beta release of the operating system, the beta version of the vendor's product will be functional upon it" and "six months after the beta release or two months after the initial final release of the operating system, whichever comes later, the production version of the vendor's product will be functional upon the final release of the operating system." Then, you can tie dollar values to these deliverables so the vendor has a financial incentive to maintain their product.

- The vendor promises that the product will work with a critical outsourced process that you were unable to test. You can help close this gap much as with operating systems. Assign measurable deliverables such as "after purchase, the vendor and the outsourcer will be connected and within three months will have the ability to transfer user, date/time, and action data in logs" (for a log management outsourcer) or "within one month, the vendor's product will be able to send start/stop time data, ticket numbers, and detail to the outsourcer who will integrate into billing" (for a billing outsourcer).

7.1.2 Price

You may be wondering why price hasn't been a factor up until now. After all, most systems that help you assess technology work out a price-per-feature calculation to help you maximize your value. However, when it comes to working with vendors, it's very difficult to put a value on things like trust and responsiveness and the attempt often results in more argument than it's worth. With this approach, by the time you finally get to this stage of the process, you have a few choices, any of which can be viewed as "good enough." As any of these options will meet your needs, you are in a great position with respect to negotiating price.

Most vendor choices will fall into one of the three categories. The open source options will tend to have no negotiable price at all, so the only factor is cost of implementation and ownership. The commoditized options are also somewhat nonnegotiable as in normal quantities you are likely to just buying something off the Internet with a credit card. However, the traditional vendor option is what you are more likely to experience. Here, you either buy a product and pay for yearly support or you pay a recurring subscription. Fortunately, in these situations, the prices are extremely flexible. These business models have extremely high profit margins so it is usually not too hard to negotiate with the vendor's sales person to lower the price to approach that of the next preferred option.

For example, suppose you settle on three options in the final analysis. You have three overall weighted scores and three initial quotes from them and three estimated operating costs. As you can't negotiate cost but have to include it as a factor, the math can get a bit tricky.

	Name		
	Agis	Babrius	Callinus
Normalized score (%)	70	65	55
Annual price	$50,000	$40,000	$20,000
Annual cost	$5,000	$4,500	$2,500

Clearly, you want Agis, but Callinus is only half the price and the difference between a 70% ideal match and a 55% may not be so bad. At this point, your price discussion should be to indirectly use the prices for Babrius and Callinus to see if you can drive that $50,000 price downward. If you can get some price movement, you win. If you can't, you can just move to Babrius, which meets almost all your needs and is 20% less. To do this, you need to determine price targets.

A price target is the value determined by the team that, if the price were to be at the value, the process would be over and that vendor would be selected. There are many ways to do this, but in the interests of simplicity, it often works to use the normalized score against the highest priced item. This process is fast and simple, but it is particularly vulnerable to top-end pinning. Another option is to do the same based on the lowest price, but this one is vulnerable to pinning at the bottom of the price range. The two processes work as follows.

7.1.3 Top-End Price Targeting

With top-end targeting, you take the highest price you were given and the difference between that and the next lowest normalized score to figure out how much of a discount you need. In the above example, there is a 5% difference between Agis and Babrius. Thus, if you can carve 5% off of Agis's price + cost, the two options are more or less equivalent. This gets you a rough estimate of feature value without wasting all the time going through each feature and assigning dollar-based numerical values. A feature-based approach is prone to argumentation and artificial manipulation to get the final result in line with expectation.

The math works as follows. Agis has a price + cost value of $55,000, and Babrius has one of $44,500. They are 5% different; 5% of $55,000 is $2,750. So, in this example, if you can get the vendor to knock off $2,750, it's worth buying. Thus, you try to negotiate the price for Agis down to $47,250. Clearly, you won't start by asking this. You might ask them to drop as low as $40,000 and point to the price of Babrius as justification. You might point to Babrius and say "let's split the difference" and ask for $45,000. It doesn't matter how you do this, all that matters is that you get the price below $47,500.

This is, of course, not much of a price difference, because of the top-end pinning problem. This problem is addressed by using a different method.

7.1.4 Bottom-End Price Targeting

With bottom-end targeting, you look at the cheapest option and figure out how expensive an idealized solution should be if all features were equal. To do this, simply divide the lowest price + cost by its normalized score. In this example, looking at Callinus, you'd just divide $22,500 by 0.55 and wind up with a price target of $40,909. You then go to the Agis vendor and point out that Callinus has enough ability to meet your needs, but it's not the one you want. See if you can get the price down and once it drops below $41,000 (to keep things simple), you can feel like you got a reasonably good deal.

7.1.5 Edge Cases

Now, clearly, these two methods can fail spectacularly in certain situations. The most common are when extremely expensive vendors are in contention with extremely cheap ones. Suppose the situation were, instead, as follows:

	Name		
	Demodocus	Epimenides	Hedyle
Normalized score (%)	70	65	55
Annual price	$500,000	$50,000	$5,000
Annual cost	$10,000	$8,500	$4,000

In this case, your top end price target would be $510,000 minus 5% of $510,000 or $484,500. Your bottom-end price target would be $9,000 divided by 55% minus the annual operating cost or $6,363. It is extremely unlikely that you will get Demodocus to drop anywhere near $6,363. It is also extremely unlikely that you would convince your management to spend an extra $450,000 to get a mere 5% additional in features.

A rough rule of thumb is that prices can be flexible within a 25% range. You may well be able to negotiate Demodocus down to $375,000 but below that is extremely unlikely.

In these situations, you should double-check that you've fully captured the cost. It is quite possible that there are hidden costs in the Epimenides and Hedyle options so the annual cost isn't properly reflected here. If Hedyle is more difficult to use and requires an additional person or two to maintain, you have to factor in the salary or hourly costs in the price. It may be that Demodocus comes with an extremely high Rhodium-level support where people will teleport to your office to fix problem, but Epimenides is bundled with only Lead support where you must get technical support via carrier pigeon and post card. By streamlining both options at "Gold," it may be that their total (price + cost) will come most in line with one another.

Once you've adjusted the prices to capture everything you can think of, if they are still more than 25% out of range with one another, odds are you'll just pick the middle option and move on with life. Always remember that the goal is to get a working solution. You're not out to beat up a vendor or get the absolute lowest price possible. You need to solve a problem and, by this point in the analysis, any of them will work. Negotiations with management and the vendor can take longer than the initial assessment run and each day you delay is another day that faster-moving companies will use to out-compete you.

That said, some negotiation will be required. Things that you should consider in this phase are in the next section.

7.1.6 Negotiation

Over the years, much has been written about negotiation. It is impossible to cover in the course of one small section of one small book what others have spent entire careers and multiple books exploring and explaining. If you wish to know more about negotiation, pick up a copy of *Getting to Yes* by Roger Fisher and William Ury (Penguin Books; 3rd edition, 2011). The remainder of this section will attempt to create a quick thumbnail sketch of the topic.

Keep in mind that the point of negotiation is to get a *fair* price, not the best one. If you beat up a vendor too much in the negotiation phase, renewal prices will likely be much higher than they otherwise would have been and your actual service levels will be lower than you'd like. Also, if the vendor is a particularly weak negotiator and every client beats them up on price, they may not survive as a business, which means that you'd have to pick another vendor in a year or two anyway. To win in the long term, you must play fair in the short term.

The key to negotiation is to consider your Best Alternative To Negotiated Agreement (BATNA). If you can't get the agreement you want, your best alternative will be another option on your list. In the running example, if Demodocus won't move on price, talk to Epimenides. After all, that solution is almost as good and a solution you have a lot better than one that you don't.

That said, there is more to negotiation than mere price, and there is more to pricing than a single or yearly purchase. Many solutions are available with a high initial cost and a lower long-term support/maintenance cost. A common model is to set the price of support at 20% of the initial price but increasingly in the technology space, support is not included with the first year purchase price. Thus, a product that costs $100,000 would have a $20,000 yearly cost. So, the first year cost is $120,000 and every year after the first year is $20,000. In your simplified price calculation, odds are that you've looked at a multiyear term. Over three years, this solution would cost $120,000 + $20,000 + $20,000 or $160,000. Thus, the annual price would be $53,333. However, if you extended the agreement to five years, the annual price drops to $40,000. Extending negotiation to include both price and time frame can add flexibility. So, if you promise to sign a three-year contract instead of a one year, you may see that price range suddenly become more flexible. This approach helps both with the figures that you'll present to management and with the ultimate price that you pay over the contract period.

As long as you work your assessment gaps into the long-term contract as exit scenarios, there is little risk to the multiyear term

Another area in which to negotiate is around service levels. This was alluded to in the discussion around support levels, but true service levels come in multiple flavors. In addition to support, you can look at service-level agreements and nonmonetary restrictions put on your ability to use the solution.

If you are negotiating support to reduce cost, be careful to not accept a level of support that will not allow you to respond to business-critical events. One common area of negotiation with appliance-based solutions is to put a premium support contract on a single piece of equipment versus just buying two so you have a spare in case something goes wrong. For software-only options, you can sometimes negotiate getting a higher support level for a lower price if you have a test environment and can demonstrate a culture of testing so the vendor knows that the support is less likely to be used.

Service-level agreements (SLAs) are more common with cloud-based offerings. These agreements are often presented as a way to guarantee your business an acceptable level of service, but in almost every instance, they are written to protect the vendor, not the customer. Things to negotiate here involve time to resolution and compensation for events. SLAs commonly have language that restricts remuneration to only those fees paid in a service period. Thus, if you are paying $5,000 per month for a business-critical service that goes down for an entire month, you may only get back $5,000 even if your business experienced a much higher loss. SLAs often also give the vendor a full business day to resolve issues which can be a problem if they work five days a week but you are a 24×7 shop.

The SLA is often presented for review and signing after the price contracts are signed. This is not to your benefit. If there will be an SLA in place, demand it during the negotiation process. This will allow you to rework the SLA to your advantage and present it along with a counter offer on price. If they refuse to move on price, accept a higher service level in exchange. If that's not acceptable to them, you have more leverage to get them to adjust the process. Similar approaches can be taken to NDAs, specifically with respect to how they handle your data after the agreement is terminated. By adding additional burdens here, particularly for cloud vendors, you can communicate to the vendor what you expect in terms of service.

Another nonfinancial point of negotiation is that of mixed use. This is typically used to get a free development or test environment (or both) so you can test changes without affecting production. In some cases, though, you can mix use across business units or even outside of the company and let your employees use the technology at home. This can dramatically improve your per-license rate and make the deal look better to the accountants. However, you should be careful that the price reduction doesn't become artificial. Each license in the calculation must have a reasonable chance of actually being used.

Finally, you can often negotiate bonus items such as training classes, access to beta software, or API documentation. These are often zero cost items to the vendor but can provide high value to your organization. These nonfinancial items can be hard to present positively to management, but if you revisit your weighted calculations, you may find that the normalized score will shift up and the cost calculation will shift down as a result of these negotiated changes. If that happens, recalculate the price targets and the value of the deal should become more apparent.

7.1.7 Negotiation Processes

The negotiation process that works best for vendors comes straight out of *Getting to Yes*. This process is based on Fisher and Ury's principles:

1. Separate the people from the problem.
2. Focus on interests, not positions.
3. Invent options for mutual gain.
4. Insist on using objective criteria.
5. Know your BATNA (Best Alternative To Negotiated Agreement).

The process that you've seen thus far has armed you for principles 1, 4, and 5. By going through the assessment, you have isolated people from the problem, identified objective criteria, and identified "fall back" vendors for your BATNA. You have also identified areas in which you can invent new options for mutual gain, but you may need to explore this piece a bit further.

Unlike higher risk and more emotional negotiations, vendors are often less amenable to negotiating with invented options. After all, you are dealing with people whose take-home pay is completely dependent on how much they can get you to spend. So, while there can certainly be areas in which both groups can benefit, if they don't directly help the sales person, such options are unlikely to be considered. Other than the suggestions in the previous section, it's usually only worth seriously exploring this third principle if you are dealing directly with an owner in the company or a particularly young (market-wise) vendor. These vendors are starving for market share and are far more interested in deals like:

- If I help you write up a case study, can I get 10% off?
- If I demo your product to my customers and they buy, can I get an extra $1,000 off at renewal?
- I need your product to do X, but it doesn't. If I write that functionality, can you maintain it?

Be aware, though, that if you pursue that avenue, it will be your burden to track the agreement as the vendor will likely have no process to do so. If the cost of this burden exceeds that of the discounts, it may not be worth your time pursuing this effort.

So, for this process, you are really focused on the second principle—Focus on interests.

Truth is key. You know what you want and need from the product. You need your problem to go away. You want to use certain features to simplify your life. You also know what the vendor needs. They need more customers to help their long-term viability and they need a purchase to improve their short-term cash flow.

So, in the end, the negotiation process is going to focus on identifying how much cash the vendor needs to make them feel good about cash flow, how long an agreement is needed to make them feel good about their market viability, and how much time and money you are willing to commit to the process.

It is usually best to sit down with the winning vendor and show them the top three choices and the prices they have presented to you. Explain to them that you have selected their product, but they need to get their prices down to the range of the other two. Alternatively, you can choose to negotiate with the bottom choice and see if they can add capabilities to their offering and provide the same capabilities as the winner but at the lower price. However, that is less of a vendor negotiation and more focused on true partnership and will not be explored in this book.

It is imperative that the sales person understands that their sales job is done and that you are now in negotiation. If they attempt to continue selling to you, presenting their option in comparison to the two competitors, gently remind them that they've already won and you are just interested in discussing price. If they need to be reminded three times, end the discussion and pick it up another day. If the sales person continues to push on features and not discuss flexibility on price, it may be time to exercise your BATNA and move along to another vendor.

If the sales person is willing to be flexible on price, keep the focus on your chosen pricing target. Do not disclose what it is but point out shortcomings of the product or service as it relates to your needs. Avoid the often overwhelming tendency to mention to the vendor that their competition provides additional capabilities. That just shifts the discussion back to selling which doesn't help anybody.

By focusing on your needs and how you will use the product, you can negotiate from a position of strength. After all, no vendor can rightly claim to understand your needs as a business better than you do. All they can do is claim to understand the product or service and, since you did actual tests with it, you likely understand it as well as they do.

Remember that price is based on value, but the initial asking price is based on market averaging. One product may be worth $100,000 to one person, but if another person will only use 80% of its capabilities, it is only worth $80,000 to them. Try to convey this to the vendor to get a reduction. Keep the discussion focused on numbers below your price target and, eventually, once you hit that number, it's time to stop negotiating and sign the final paperwork.

Negotiation isn't always straightforward, and you may need to go a few rounds with the vendor to make this work. Before you start, decide how much time it is worth to get the price reduction you are after. For smaller purchases for a medium-sized business, this may only be worth half a day. For large purchases in a multinational organization, you may need to devote a few weeks to negotiation.

Then, as you negotiate, keep a spreadsheet. This spreadsheet should list all the data you need for each of your final candidates and give you the ability to record the discounts that you are negotiating. Each time you enter a discount, record the date, the reason for the discount, and the person who offered it to you. Then, when you're in the final stages, you can compare the exact numbers you have to those that the vendor puts on the contract. It is sadly common for certain discounts to disappear once the final agreement is presented to be signed.

Issue	Request	Justification	Time Value
No support for Windows 8	−$10,000	Lack of Windows 8 support will slow down deployment and increase opportunity costs during the delay	2 h
Encryption key stored in C:/Temp/	−$5,000/year	The lack of proper protection of encryption keys necessitates additional software to protect the disk. This software costs $5,000/year	1 h
No redundant option available	−$15,000	The network architecture changes needed to support redundant routing requires additional equipment and licensing	2 h
Solution requires SQL Server 2005	−$5,000	Organization already upgraded to 2008. Solution will require a dedicated database instead of connecting to the existing farm	1 h
Operations procedures conflict with current employee processes	−$30,000	Adapting processes to use solution will cost a significant amount of time and the change itself will not provide value	4 h

If you've burned through 80% of your allocated negotiated time and haven't gotten to an agreement, tell them so. Just let them know that you need to have an agreement by the final date and if it's not an agreement to do business, it will be an agreement not to do business and you will go to the next competitor on the list. Make sure they understand that you do not want to do this, but you also cannot spend an infinite amount of time on negotiation. In almost all cases, you find the vendor coming down to meet your target and you can move on to production. This is particularly true at the end of your vendor's quarter or year. This is when the sales people have to hit their goals or risk losing their jobs and/or bonuses, so prices can suddenly get a lot more flexible.

In those few cases where the price simply can't be dropped enough, you must decide to either raise your target or move to your next vendor (BATNA). If the team decides to raise the target to meet what the vendor is asking, do so and finish up. If, however, you actually do need to talk to the next vendor, the negotiation process starts over. Once again, decide how long you can spend in negotiation, cut the first vendor from the list and recalculate your price targets. Then, contact the second vendor on the list, tell them that negotiations with the first vendor fell through, and ask if they can be flexible enough on price to help you hit your new price target.

If you manage to go through your entire short list and not come to an agreement, consider that you may not be negotiating in good faith or you may not actually need the solution in the first place. Some problems can be lived with and are simply not worth the cost of solving. It can be quite irritating to halt negotiation at this point in the process, but beware the fallacy of sunk costs. The money and time that you have put into the process has been spent. Further expense in pursuit of a solution that will not provide enough value for the money simply results in more money being lost.

PHASE 8

Production

8.1 PRODUCTION

Once the chosen solution is in production, it is time to start preparing for renewal. While this book does not cover the entire vendor management process, it is important to close the loop so you may continue the assessment process at renewal time. This includes identifying when the renewal period will begin so you can build systems to collect data that you can use later. It is common for vendors to take advantage of renewal periods to increase the price, as it is always difficult to move away from an existing solution. Because they know that there will be an increased cost of change the longer you use their solution, they can keep boosting the price slightly each cycle.

Before a product or service is implemented in production, you should first think about how you will know whether or not it is working properly. There are many metrics that can be used, from uptime calculations to speed of response. Remember though that you are trying to solve a problem, so think about the problem that you're solving and how to measure that. You can measure on either side of the problem, either verifying that the problem exists or that the solution is working.

At the very least, by the time you finish implementing the solution, whatever metric you are using to measure your problem should show a great change. For example, if you are implementing a replacement Help Desk system, you should see a reduction in the amount of time that tickets stay open or an increase in customer satisfaction levels. If you are purchasing SSD drives for enterprise-wide deployment, you should see a faster application load-time that results in increased performance within those teams. If you are implementing a database firewall, you should see the absence of metrics. In other words, as it is a purely defensive technology, it should provide protection without causing interruption.

As you collect and tune these metrics, consider building "metrics engines." These are automated systems that collect and store your metrics. They are commonly built into monitoring packages, but there is more to metrics than network statistics. Other automated systems consist of report generators that are often bundled into systems, data that appears in audit logs, and systems that issue alerts via SNMP or WMI. You should also consider manually collected data that is commonly collected and presented at meetings. All you have to do is identify where these metrics originate and feed them back into a single source connected with the vendor. In highly mature organizations, this could be a dedicated database owned by their vendor management team. In less mature organizations, it can simply be a shared folder into which everything is dumped.

As the product goes into production, maintain a list of things that go wrong. This can be as minor as unclear documentation costing your team a few hours or as major as a key feature not being available until a future release. Put down estimates for how much that issue cost your organization. Also, track the dates that the problems occurred and the people involved, so you can go back to them for more information should it be needed. Maintain this list up until the vendor contacts you for renewal.

Then, when you're halfway through your agreement period, reconvene the original team for an afternoon. Go through the collected data and your original analysis. First, determine where you went wrong in your initial analysis. No one is perfect, so there will almost always be room for improvement. Understanding where those areas are will help you improve the accuracy or speed of future vendor assessment projects.

Next, review the metrics that you've gathered up until this point and verify that the original problem has been addressed by the solution. See what, if anything, remains to be done before the product or service can be considered "completely implemented." The goal is to remove any power from the vendor to say "sure you had problems, but you've not been using our product correctly."

This fallback position is common because information technology is so complex that almost no one ever uses it the same way, so every time a customer complains to a vendor about the product or service, the vendor tries to convince them that they're using it wrong and they should buy training or a tuning process. While there is nothing wrong with a tuning or training process, there is a problem when a vendor's response to a problem is to ask for more money. By this point, you and the vendor should be working as a team to maximize your success.

Once you know whether the product is working for you, you can begin preparing for vendor "tickles." Vendors, whether they win or lose a process, create "tickler files" so they can call or e-mail you at specific intervals and try to get you to renew or replace your existing solution. By having the data on hand, you can quickly determine whether or not you are looking to make a change at renewal time and what else you might be looking for.

If you plan to keep what you have, you may use your collected data to negotiate the renewal costs, again from a perspective of how well the solution meets your needs. Just go back to the negotiation process and work with the vendor. The only difference is that if they can't hit your target, you must choose to either pay their price or start the entire assessment process over again. Figure out what the assessment process and reimplementation would cost you and if it exceeds the cost of the renewal, it is likely better to just renew...assuming the current solution actually works.

If the current solution is not meeting your needs, it is time to restart the assessment process. Go back to the beginning of the process, build your list of candidates, rapidly filter them, go through the assessment and scoring process, and begin negotiation with the winner. This process should be much faster and easier than the first time, as you have been living with a solution from that vendorspace for a period of time. This would significantly decrease your learning curve and will help you pick the features that truly matter.

Conclusion

9.1 CONCLUSION

Your first vendor assessment using this process will likely feel awkward. If you are not used to a data-driven approach to making decisions, it will be slow and inefficient. As you practice, though, it will get much faster. Think about the first time you tried to drive a car. Odds are that you are much more comfortable with the process now and get where you're going a lot faster than when you were walking everywhere. Gaining business skills is a lot like this. However, there is a lot less social pressure around continual improvement in the business world, so there is a strong tendency to just give up when things feel inefficient. If you want to succeed, you have to keep at it. Here are some things to keep in mind as you start your vendor assessment practice.

9.1.1 Keep Your Eye on the Prize

Nothing kills this process faster than forgetting that your goal is to solve a business problem. As soon as you fall into the trap of thinking you are going to use this process to pick the perfect vendor, everything will take longer and you'll likely wind up with a poorer solution. If you try to bite off too much at once, often by solving too many business problems with a single solution, complexity rises and failure becomes much more likely.

Finally, if you enter into the process trying to justify your existing vendor, you may well also fail. Data driven approaches exist to help you find flaws, not to help you defend preconceived notions. The more you try to use this process for defense, the more you'll find yourself corrupting the model. Because this model uses Lean/Agile methods, it is particularly vulnerable to corruption. Lean/Agile methods presume that everyone on the team shares goals and is mature enough to talk through issues. The efficiency of the system is gained by eliminating heavier time-wasting processes, some of which are used to help resolve problems. Instead of building these checks directly into the system, look for the following issues as evidence of process breakdown:

- Drifting away from the time-driven nature of the model often indicates that the assessment is in danger of analysis paralysis. You can get enough data to make a decision long before you have enough data to satisfy your curiosity. The business does not thrive on satisfied curiosity.
- Adding more time to the process for one vendor and not for others often indicates that you have a favorite and are tilting the process to their advantage. This is unfair and will likely result in a poorer overall solution and a higher price to maintain it. If you find yourself doing this, identify why you like the vendor and try to determine if you've missed features or hidden costs.
- Adjusting weights beyond simply using twos, threes, and fours (or halves, thirds, and quarters) often indicates that you are manipulating the process to force your preferred vendor into a winning state. Make sure that the entire team agrees with the weighted variables before you run your final calculations.
- Using the six variables from the Parkerian Hexad without thinking about them indicates that you are trying to take a cookie-cutter approach. Think about your assessment dimensions and make sure that you are getting full coverage for the issues you face. Just because these variables work fairly well for me doesn't mean that they are ideal for your specific needs. They may work, but there may be better ways to think about your problem.

9.1.2 Avoiding Vendor Manipulation

Vendors are at their best when their products or services help you solve your problems. However, they are their worst when their sales are particularly weak or particularly strong. Strong vendors are less inclined to negotiate with you or provide you the highest level of customer service. Weak vendors are more inclined to fudge the information they give you, as they must make sales to survive. Vendors tend to cycle between being strong and being weak several times throughout their life cycle. Knowing where they are in their cycle can be critical in identifying how much time to spend on the deep dive and negotiation phases of the assessment.

If the vendor is public, keep an eye on their stock price and if it is 25+% higher or lower than the two year average for the company, be aware of how that might affect the vendor's behavior toward you. If they are private, it's a bit more difficult, but you can often find out what the previous years' revenues have been, what this year's goal is, and how close the company is to meet the goal by just asking your sales person.

Also, keep in mind that the vendors benefit greatly from "lock in." The harder they can make it for you to move to another solution, the more likely they are to get renewals. Some vendors manage this by price, setting yearly renewals to 20% of the initial cost. Some vendors do this technologically and build tight integration into their products, so migrating away from them is extremely difficult. Other vendors trust in strong relationships to keep you buying from them.

However, the fundamental truth is that as soon as the vendor stops providing solutions to your problems, it's time to change. Cheap renewals of products that don't meet your current business needs are, in fact, extremely expensive because the cost of operation increases dramatically. Technology that is "sticky" that no longer meets your needs is also much more costly, as you have to use resources to keep the technology running and use even more resources to kludge processes around the technology to work around its flaws. Finally, a free vendor-provided lunch that ropes you into an additional year for an expensive technology when there are cheaper options is the most expensive lunch you can have.

Where possible, try to decouple your solutions from one another, so they can be swapped out easily. If systems communicate via standards such as Syslog or SNMP, you can keep things fairly isolated and be able to swap vendors at will. The most costly portion of a vendor change should be retraining your people, not decoupling hard-coded technological processes. This could involve additional costs to the vendor, contracts with a third-party training firm, and the loss of productivity during the training period.

Finding the right balance can be tricky, but once done, you should be able to review vendors once per year, using this same process, and easily pivot from one to another based on business needs. After all, if the vendors are doing the job, they will have adjusted their offering to meet your evolving needs and no other vendor in the market will even come close to being able to serve you as effectively.

9.2 FINAL WORDS

Life has, as one of its core principles, constant and accelerating change. Business is no different. Living beings react to this by evolving to meet new challenges and dropping features that no longer provide competitive advantage. Business, in general, hasn't done a good job of figuring this out. This means that by just taking the initial steps to being nimble with respect to how your business works, you can grow by leaps and bounds. At a business level, profits should increase. At a personal level, you should see increased promotion opportunities.

However, you can't get something for nothing and the trade-off to embracing change is feeling increased pain. Others in your organization may not buy into the process, so you'll have to start small and have numerous discussions about what you're doing and why. You may make poor decisions because you didn't ask the right questions, so you'll have to analyze failure and adjust your process so it works better each time you use it. Most importantly, you have to keep moving.